THE NATURE, PRACTICE AND HISTORY OF ART

BY

H. VAN BUREN MAGONIGLE

FELLOW OF THE AMERICAN INSTITUTE OF ARCHITECTS, ASSOCIATE OF THE NATIONAL ACADEMY OF DESIGN,
ROTCH TRAVELLING SCHOLAR IN ARCHITECTURE, PAST PRESIDENT OF THE ASSOCIATION OF
THE ALUMNI OF THE AMERICAN ACADEMY IN ROME, PAST PRESIDENT OF THE ARCHI-
TECTURAL LEAGUE OF NEW YORK, VICE-PRESIDENT OF THE NATIONAL
SCULPTURE SOCIETY, AUTHOR OF "ARCHITECTURAL RENDER-
ING IN WASH," "THE RENAISSANCE," ETC., ETC.

ILLUSTRATED

CHARLES SCRIBNER'S SONS

NEW YORK · LONDON

1927

E
T   Q
V

PREFACE

SEVERAL years ago the able head of one of our schools of design expressed to me a regret that the future patrons of art in America, the young men and women in high school and college, were growing up in virtual ignorance of art as art, as a source of pleasure, as an influence upon life, or as an expression of life, and suggested that as the then President of the Architectural League I do something about it. In the enthusiasm of the moment it seemed that a book was the thing to do and that I might attempt it. As it took shape I determined not to make it strictly a text-book for school use only, but so to treat it that it might be acceptable and useful to the laity at large, and it assumed its present form.

I am conscious that it bears the scars inevitable in the conflict between the claims of a busy professional life and the desire to contribute to a more wide-spread knowledge of Western art; it has been laid aside again and again and written at all sorts of odd times. But the time has come to write Finis and send it forth as it is. I am aware, too, of the audacity of an attempt to deal with so vast a subject so briefly; but there are many long books about the arts, and long books are discouraging to many people; I wanted to write a short one that might have a fair chance of being read through without too much skipping.

In selection and compression the choice of the most significant relation between an art and the period that gave it birth was of course the most difficult and delicate part of my task; as to what I have omitted, or as to the interpretation or ascription of causes, or as to conclusions, I see no other course than to assume full responsibility. It will be found that I have, particularly in the historical chapters, painted a picture consisting chiefly in high lights—but if this was enforced by brevity it also imposed a certain care in the treatment of fundamentals. It may be deemed a merit that the book is written by a practitioner, from the inside as it were; on the other hand it may be thought to have the defects of that merit.

As to the general arrangement, it seems logical to give the reader some idea of the nature and practice of art before dealing with its historical relations. The plan of making the illustrations independent of the text by their accompanying notes will be found, I hope, of practical convenience. And I take what I believe to be a pardonable pride in announcing that there is not one foot-note in the book.

Following the course I had found to be effective and helpful in other cases, I submitted the manuscript from time to time to a group of friends of varied age, experience, and education, some laymen, others engaged in the arts, and their criticisms and suggestions were of immense service; they are too many to thank all by name, but I here record my gratitude to them for their friendly offices; it is not invidious to distinguish two among them, William Jones and Ben J. Lubschez, for especial thanks for special help.

To Mrs. Magonigle I am indebted for invaluable assistance in the grouping of the illustrations; and to Mr. W. C. Brownell for the generosity with which, in reading proof, he placed at my disposal his distinguished critical faculty and the treasures of a culture mellow and sympathetic, various and profound.

H. VAN BUREN MAGONIGLE.

NEW YORK CITY,
February 6th, 1924.

CONTENTS

PART I

CONTENTS

ILLUSTRATIONS

Author's Note: *The lining-papers at the front and back of the book carry maps upon which the currents of influence in the Classic, Mediæval, and Renaissance epochs may be traced. These are based upon diagrams made by the author in 1893–94 to illustrate his lectures upon the arts of design at Cowles's Art School in Boston, which proved very useful then and should be far more so in their present form, indicating as they do not only geographical relations but, wherever practicable, the probable course the influence followed, by sea, trade route, or river valley.*

With certain exceptions, notably the first four pages, the illustrations are arranged as nearly as possible in chronological order. The measure of their importance is not that of their relative size, which was usually determined by practical considerations of arrangement, shape, and availability. The titles under them are designed to amplify and supplement the text and relieve it of the burden of dates and similar information so apt to pull a reader up and to check the swing of the narrative.

The reader's convenience has been studied by so placing them on the page that in no instance is it necessary to turn the book. Nor are there any reference notes in the text to the pictures, even though in many cases they have been chosen to elucidate some portion of it, because a reader's attention is disturbed and diverted by such references. But by merely going over the illustrations in their order and reading the notes beneath them, he may gather a general and orderly impression of the framework of that vast temple of beauty in which so many artists have labored and to whose service they have consecrated their lives.

ILLUSTRATIONS

xiii

ILLUSTRATIONS

ILLUSTRATIONS

ILLUSTRATIONS

ILLUSTRATIONS

xvii

ILLUSTRATIONS

xviii

ILLUSTRATIONS

ILLUSTRATIONS

PART ONE

THE LAST JUDGMENT above the altar of the Sistine Chapel, begun for Pope Clement VII by MICHAEL ANGELO BUONARROTI and finished in his 67th year. Enormous in dimension, 54.6 high by 43.8 wide, the color has almost departed and has been so many times retouched by inferior hands that little of Angelo is left except the great design—chaos controlled by the hand of a master. It exhibits the exaggerations and mannerisms that crept into the work of the aging Titan.

soul of Raphael. A survey of all the works of the two men shows these contrasts running through them all. Angelo's indicates a man visited by terrible visions; Raphael's a man at peace with his material and spiritual worlds. And each exhibits a different phase of their many-sided epoch.

We pass to France of the late seventeenth and early eighteenth centuries. Jean Antoine Watteau was born in 1684, when Louis XIV, *Le Grand Monarque*, was King; a little King, who increased his stature by high-heeled shoes and an absurdly tall and voluminous wig of curled horse-hair—a King nevertheless of character and ability; the wig and the high heels are symbolic of the artificiality and pompous insincerity of the time. Louis XIV died seven years before Watteau; and before he died, the King, after a life of pleasure, became a religious devotee under the influence of Madame de Maintenon. Gloom pervaded the court; but at Louis's death the most violent reaction took place and the license and depravity of the following régime has passed into legend. Watteau was not of the court, but he is a connecting link between the two reigns. We have deliberately chosen him to illustrate our thesis because the character he reveals in his work is so at variance with all the accounts of his nature, and the very difference points the argument that no artist can fail to disclose his innermost self in his art. He was, as the world saw him, a sickly young man, a misanthrope of unstable character, a recluse constantly changing his place of abode, given to bitter and sarcastic gibes, dying of consumption at thirty-seven. And here enters the apparent contradiction which modern criticism penetrates to find the soul behind it—his work, full of phantasy, fabrics of dreams, where courtly lovers woo delicate ladies "to the sound of flute and viol" in landscapes of melting sweetness, shows not a trace of this outer man. "All men of creative genius are slaves to their own temperament. The creator whose blood is red, whose circulation is rapid, and whose muscles are strong gives birth to vigorous conceptions. . . . But the frail and sickly poet . . . shrinks from the strenuous passions and strifes of humanity . . . the suffering genius builds as a refuge a pleasure palace for his own frail soul, a world from which all elements which hurt him in the real world are absent, a fairy land of color . . . where Spring reigns eternal. . . . Such was the world which Watteau created for himself . . . and here his sick soul might find itself safe from all contact with the brutality of real life." Thus Dargenty, in his *Antoine Watteau*. Who shall say that in his work we do not find the real Watteau, the poet of delicate fancy imprisoned in the outer man like a sweet kernel in a bitter husk—a poet who could not, moreover, escape the artificiality of the age in which he lived, and all unconsciously exhibits it to us who follow?

When Watteau was nineteen years old and Louis XIV had twelve more years to live, François Boucher was born. By the time he had reached young manhood Louis XV was King of France. This child, who ascended the throne at the age of five to reign for fifty-nine years, could hardly exercise a restraining influence upon a society which concealed, beneath the most graceful manners, a profound corruption that early contaminated the young King. After the dull days of the close of his great-grandfather's rule, the court gave itself up to the extreme of voluptuous indulgence. It was into this dissolute, decadent, pleasure-seeking society that Boucher was thrown; and at the service of this society he placed an immense talent, a wealth of fancy that found utterance in exquisitely sophisticated compositions in the general vein which Watteau had made popular. Boucher was no misanthropic recluse. He swam with the stream. At

The DISPUTA, or Discussion of the Christian Faith, one of four mural paintings and a number of ceiling panels by Raffaello Sanzio, called RAPHAEL, in the Stanza della Segnatura in the Vatican. Typical of the design of Raphael, who has been aptly called "a great space-filler" and who, as a mural painter, never surpassed the quality of this work, executed in the flush of his youth as his first commission in Rome for Pope Julius II, about 1512.

PORTRAIT OF RAFFAELLO SANZIO
Painted by himself
Born at Urbino, 1483
Died at Rome, 1520

thirty-one he was a member of the Academy; at fifty-two he became Inspector of the Gobelins, the royal tapestry manufactory; at sixty-two he was made First Painter to the King; Madame de Pompadour, one of the mistresses of the King, was his friend and patroness. He died in 1770, four years before his King and master.

Here was a man upon whom, as upon Raphael, fortune smiled. No dark dreams visited him. His paintings seem to have been the natural product of a cheerful nature developed in a cheerful and congenial atmosphere. Society, during the long reigns of Louis XIV and Louis XV, had become highly organized, highly conventional, thoroughly artificial. It was not an age of individualism. It was not a society of lofty ideals; it did not wish to think—merely to be lightly amused, to be pleased. Conformity to usage, to good form, was demanded of courtier and painter alike. This society had developed a certain kind of taste, and in Watteau and Boucher it found the men who could minister to it. To this agreement of their contemporaries upon taste and style may be ascribed the substantial likeness in the work of these two men, despite the difference in their characters and their lives.

To sum up the facts we have examined: we find in France, in Italy, and in Greece, in times disparate, under social conditions widely at variance, the art of the time expressing the time, the art of the race expressing the race at that time, the art of the individual disclosing the individual. The work of Phidias and of Praxiteles is unmistakably Greek— compare it with that of the other four. The work of Angelo and of Raphael is unmistakably Italian—compare theirs with the others'. The paintings of Watteau and Boucher could only have been done by Frenchmen. The art of Phidias and of Praxiteles is absolutely that of certain periods of

Greek history, that of Angelo and Raphael could only have been produced under the conditions of their epoch in Italy, that of Watteau and Boucher only under the special influences of aristocratic life in the France of the seventeenth and eighteenth centuries.

In like manner, quite unconsciously, as such forces must act, the artists of to-day are writing the history of our time and revealing themselves and us to posterity. Poet, dramatist, architect, sculptor, painter, musician, critic, are acting in the dual capacity of creators and mirrors of our intellectual, and in large measure our material, life. If the architecture of New York of any decade should seem trivial or vulgar to posterity, it would be because the ideals of the city and of the architects of that decade were vulgar and trivial. The architecture and painting of Venice are the visible sign of the rich and luxurious life of the enlightened oligarchy that ruled her. The city of Paris shows the clear, logical mind of the French applied to the solution of problems of civic order and beauty. Scandinavian drama exhibits the morbid introspectiveness engendered by the rigors of long, dark winters in a climate almost arctic. In the American school of landscape painting is reflected the love of outdoors so typical of our nation and a fine sensitiveness to the beauty of the moods of nature; while on the other hand, the weakness of our portraiture indicates a people less interested in human beings than in the world in which they move. The Renaissance period, the time of salient personalities, was the time of great and vivid portraiture by men intensely interested in men as men.

Art is thus to be apprehended, not as something remote, outside of life or a purely decorative grace of life, with which the average man or woman, boy or girl, has no concern, unless he or she takes up the life and work of the artist as a

A composition by JEAN ANTOINE WATTEAU, from the Wallace Collection in London. He was born at Valenciennes in 1684, seven years after Louis XIV had made that city French. He died at Paris in 1721. French society of his day liked to trifle with the idea of rustic simplicity, provided it could be enjoyed with elegance. Watteau was fond of portraying also the odd characters to be found among the strolling players at the fairs and on the roads of France.

By FRANÇOIS BOUCHER, born 1703 at Paris and died there in 1770. From the Wallace Collection, London. The title is unimportant; "Shepherd and Nymph" or the names of any semi-mythical figures of romance would suffice. The figure plays a more important part in the works of Boucher than in those of Watteau. Boucher was a painter of immense ability, a great composer in his genre, a master draftsman and brushman, born into a society of trivial ambitions and ideals.

career, but, on the contrary, a part, and a very important part, of the daily life of every one of us. We should surely all like to think that we have better taste, more cultivation, than was current in that dreadful period which immediately preceded, let us say, eighteen hundred and seventy—a century or more of false taste or lack of any soever. We should hardly care to have future generations say of us what we say of the æsthetic sense of our grandparents. But let us remember that we are, all of us, layman and artist alike, unconsciously making for future generations to read, a record of our taste, of our sensitiveness to beauty and to the finer things of life. The record will be no more splendid than the quality of our generation. Art, the Recorder, is inexorable.

> "The Moving Finger writes; and having writ,
> Moves on; nor all your Piety nor Wit
> Shall lure it back to cancel half a Line
> Nor all your Tears wipe out a Word of it."

It is of vital importance for us all to learn as much as we may of the art of this world we live in. He who understands art has at his command a means of communication with the African savage painting his shield, or the Indians of the pueblos weaving their blankets; he speaks the language of the Japanese connoisseur; he is at home in the depths of China and India and in all the far places of the earth; and all lands and all ages are his. In these pages I shall try to convey a clear idea of the nature, practice, and history of art, in the briefest possible compass. We are to deal especially with the three arts of Architecture, Sculpture, and Painting and in a limited degree with the divers arts that derive from them. The origins and the psychology of the arts of the East differ so widely from those of the Western world that they cannot be conveniently included here, although the arts of China and Japan are immensely important and have strongly affected the work of many Western masters, notably James McNeill Whistler. The reader will find *Epochs of Chinese and Japanese Art,* by Ernest Fenollosa, a brilliant and fascinating book.

CHAPTER II

THE QUALITIES COMMON TO ALL FORMS OF ART

Fundamental Principles — Design — Proportion — Balance — Symmetry — Rhythm — Pattern — Spotting or Notan — Harmony — Contrast — Taste — Style and Styles — The Grand Style — The Intimate Style — Tradition and its Value — Imagination — Beauty the Touchstone.

ALL works of art, whether poems, musical compositions, works of architecture, or sculpture, or painting, will be found upon analysis to have fundamental traits, qualities, principles, in common, such as: Design, Proportion, Balance, Symmetry, Rhythm, Pattern, Harmony, Contrast, Taste, Style, Beauty. Some of these are more evident in some forms of artistic expression than in others—as for example, Pattern, which is more evident in the art of textile weaving than in Music, although in the larger sense Pattern is to be found in Music as well. Style and Beauty are the products of Design, Proportion, Balance, Symmetry, Rhythm, Pattern, Harmony, Contrast; and Taste is the selective quality which combines these elements in such a manner as to produce Style and Beauty.

While these traits or principles are more evident in some forms of expression than in others, no work of art soever can exist without Design, for Design is the means by which the underlying beautiful thought that is art, the underlying aim or intention, is to be made manifest to other minds than that of the artist. Design establishes the proportion of the parts to the whole or to each other, arranges the elements so that they are in Balance or are Symmetrical to each other, disposes them in such relations that they produce a sense of Rhythm or cadenced spacing, and create a Pattern, more or less obvious, more or less concealed, as the designer desires.

It is evident that while Design must exist in a work of art, it may not be a successful or an interesting, a tasteful or a beautiful Design. The original aim may have been admirable, but the Proportion, Balance, Rhythm, or Pattern, may be badly worked out or combined. On the other hand, the primary thought may have been commonplace, and no amount of ingenuity in the arrangement of Proportion and the rest can make its expression really interesting or distinguished. We have defined art as a beautiful thought made audible or visible; but we must recognize that there are degrees of beauty in thought, as well as in expression.

In beginning a Design that is to make the thought visible or audible, whether a cathedral, a picture, a book, or a symphony, the first thing to do is to establish general Proportions: of a cathedral, relative length, width, and height; of a picture, width to height; and of a book, that portion of the field with which it deals that it is proposed to cover. The second step is to determine, tentatively at least, the proportions of the parts to the whole, as: in the façade of the cathedral, the size and shape of the doors and windows; in a landscape picture, the amount of sky in proportion to the earth shown; in a book, the content and relative importance of the chapters. The third—and this is a process that goes on throughout the act of producing a work of art—is to adjust the proportions of the parts to each other until they are brought into a Harmony as nearly satisfactory to the artist as may be. Proportion, then, may be defined as the relation, as to size, quantity, value, or importance, between the parts and the whole, and of the parts to each other. Proportion is also a positive quality, rather than relative, inherent in

22

the whole as a whole; that is to say, irrespective of the relations of parts, the whole may be a well-proportioned shape or the reverse.

To balance is to place, or keep, in equilibrium. In a work of art, Balance is a very subtle and difficult thing to describe. It is, of course, arrived at very differently in the several arts. In Music, volume of sound would be balanced by volume of sound perhaps of another nature or quality so as to produce equilibrium. Balance, in Architecture, in Sculpture, and in Painting, is attained by the counterbalancing of one mass by another, whether of color or of form; by the opposition of lines; by such disposition of the elements of the Pattern as to stabilize them and leave them in a state of apparent rest. Symmetry is, of course, the most obvious form of Balance; when two objects, just alike, are placed on either side of an axis and in the same relation to that axis, they are symmetrically disposed, and they exactly Balance. Balance may, therefore, be considered as referring principally to bodies or shapes unequal in mass, or color, or volume.

Rhythm is a system of accentuation of certain parts or elements of a Design to produce, in Architecture, Sculpture, or Painting, the equivalent of musical Rhythm, or measured movement such as we see in dancing. It is also an arrangement of lines and masses in such relations as to produce the effect of a flowing transition from one line or mass to another. In Architecture one of the many forms of Rhythm is an arrangement of windows in groups recurring at intervals, as: two windows grouped—a space—three windows grouped—a space—two windows again—a space—three windows—space—and again two windows. We say that the windows are rhythmically spaced in such a case. In Figure Painting or Sculpture another form of Rhythm, and only one of the many, would be an arrangement of the lines of the bodies, limbs, and drapery, so that the lines or the masses of light and shade flow into each other, or repeat each other, and tend to unite, to tie together in the professional phrase, the entire composition. Repeated line is one of the elements of Rhythm.

Pattern may be defined as the distribution of masses of color or form in agreeable space- or mass-relations. It is also, used in another sense, the interweaving or disposition of lines in such a manner as to produce definite figures in which the lines either count as lines, or as defining the outlines of shapes or figures. But it is in the former sense it is to be chiefly understood as applying in this discussion. Akin to Pattern is the term Spotting—approximately what the Japanese call Notan. The term is almost self-explanatory, and means the placing of the important masses in a drawing or painting with relation to each other. It has an intimate relation to Balance.

Harmony is an agreeable and satisfying arrangement of line, of color, of light and shade, of mass, of Balance, Rhythm, Proportion—all the elements of a Design.

Contrast is the opposition of light to dark, width to height, great dimensions to small, length to brevity, a staccato accent to a measured cadence, and the like. The elements of a Contrast may be either harmonious or inharmonious with each other.

In dealing with these principles, definitions cannot be exact, for the qualities interfuse and partake sometimes of the characteristics of another, sometimes of several, and there is thus between each and the others a shadowy borderland that defies definition. And, after all, after the most searching analysis and the most acute definition of the elements of a work of art, the all-essential spirit of Beauty in it eludes all analysis, all definition. Of Beauty, I decline to attempt any definition. I am with Denman Ross in this; and recommend his *Theory of Pure Design* to the serious student who wishes to know more about Balance, Rhythm, and Harmony.

Taste, in the artist, is that selective judgment which combines the elements of Design into a beautiful whole; it is thus, in the artist, an active quality. Taste, in the observer, is a passive quality; it is the trained judgment which perceives the beautiful or admirable qualities the artist has given a work of art. Taste in the artist or in the observer is not necessarily native or instinctive. It may be cultivated to the most sensitive degree from beginnings, or apparent natural aptitudes, the least promising. Its standards change from decade to decade, from century to century. It may be broadly stated that at periods when Taste is narrow and exclusive it is usually at low ebb, and that when it is catholic, broad, and inclusive of all that is best in the world, it is in its best estate. A highly cultivated taste embraces much that one less developed rejects. It is quite impossible to define Good Taste and Bad Taste; usually good taste is one's own, and bad taste the other fellow's. The student of art, whether layman or professional, is in better case just now than at any other period of American history because Taste is broad and all-inclusive, and facilities for the study and comparison of the arts of the world have been multiplied; and the formation of a sound and cultivated taste is, therefore, possible to any one who will take the trouble to acquire it by constant, serious study of what, by the test of time and the opinion of the best judges, are considered as the masterpieces of each of the great epochs of artistic history, in Architecture, Sculpture, Painting, Literature, Music—all the forms of artistic expression.

A thoughtful analysis of the past will reveal the artist as responding to a pressure exerted upon his faculties by the movement of events in the society of which he was a part, and all artists reacting in a generally similar manner to that pressure; that reaction, that response, issued in Style. The pressure was the result of a general and quite uniformly distributed Taste, of that general agreement upon modes of life and thought which is the flower and the mark of a homogeneous and ordered social state. We must differentiate between Style and styles; by the latter we mean the so-called historic styles or periods. Style is difficult to define in the sense in which the artist uses it. We may say that when a thing has Style it has elegance, character, distinction. When a woman is described as having style, every woman knows what is meant; it does not mean that her clothes are necessarily in the latest fashion; it is some felicity in the choice of color, of material, something in the cut, and, above all, something in the way she wears them. Style is above the fashion of the moment. The note of Style runs through all the best work of all the great periods. There are a few men in the history of art whose conceptions are so far above the average, whose powers of expression are so adequate to their conceptions, whose work has such power such distinction, such lofty character, that we say such men possess the Grand Style. Phidias, Dante, Bramante, Michael Angelo, Shakspere, Milton, Beethoven, are such men. Many lesser men, while failing to attain the ultimate distinction, give us beautiful things; others merely exhibit themselves as empty, pretentious, and dull; and there are many, many more who set themselves no such high goal as that of the great masters, but, like the Dutch masters such as Ver Meer of Delft, one of the greatest painters of all time confine themselves to the portrayal of simple, intimate

26

themes exquisitely wrought, and contribute to the sum of the world's beauty. To be lifted up to lofty summits by Shakspere and Angelo is a tremendous spiritual experience; but the vast average of mankind finds it difficult to breathe that atmosphere for long, and finds repose and refreshment at lesser levels with the many who possess Style, if not the Grand Style, like Robert Louis Stevenson and Jan Ver Meer.

There is an immense deal of respectable, craftsmanlike work in the world that is nevertheless quite without Imagination. Imagination does not merely mean the creation of new things or themes but means also the investiture of old or familiar themes with a new meaning, a new life. A portrait-painter without Imagination may give us the physical facts of the sitter with astounding accuracy; the physical likeness, feature for feature, may be perfect, but, lacking imagination, he is unable to divine, to imagine, the spiritual man or woman behind the veil of flesh and blood, and the picture leaves us cold. Sometimes in the columns of a newspaper we will encounter, in the midst of dull recitals of matters of fact, a story lighted up from behind as it were by a flash of Imagination. Imagination is not entirely the original beautiful thought; it is also the power to clothe the thought, and present it, in terms of interest and distinction.

We may not close this chapter without a note upon Tradition and its values. Art must develop much as language develops. No man having something to say invents a new language to express his new thought; he uses the parts of speech familiar to us all, uses the alphabet of his race, and with these simple elements in new combinations makes us burn or shiver, tremble or exult. And so each art must respect the traditions of its past and develop new things with the old sap, just as new leaves grow on old trees every

Spring. The leaf does not despise the roots hidden deep in the earth over which it quivers in the light of a new day.

And above and beyond all these attributes hovers the Spirit of Beauty, elusive, desirable, not to be defined, to whose service the artist dedicates his life, before whose shrine he lights and guards the flame of sacrifice in the hope that she may smile upon his work, giving it that last irradiation without which there is no art.

CHAPTER III

THE ARTIST

The Meaning of Artist — The Artisan — The Craftsman — Position of the
Artist in Successive Epochs — The Guilds — The Bottega — The Patron —
Simplicity of the Artist's Point of View — The Poseur and his Airs of
Mystery — The Studios of the Painter and the Sculptor — The Office of
the Architect.

THERE is current a misuse of the appellation "artist"
which it will be well to indicate, and remove at once the
misunderstanding that results from it. One hears painters
of national reputation refer to themselves and other painters as "artists" and say that So-and-so is not an artist but
a sculptor or an architect. This is, of course, merely a careless or an ignorant use of language; but its constant repetition has had the effect of lodging in the minds of the laity
the idea that an artist is only he who paints pictures.

An artist is a practitioner of any of the arts of expression.
The architect, the painter, the sculptor, musician, poet,
writer, dramatist, actor, the designer of decorative objects
of use or beauty, all are artists. The artist who paints pictures is a painter, the artist who writes or performs musical
compositions is a musician, and so on through all the arts.

Next in rank is the craftsman or the artisan in the artistic
crafts or trades, such as: wrought ironwork, bronze and
the precious metals, textile weaving and printing, stained
and painted glass, pottery, tile work, faience, stamped and
tooled leather, book printing and binding, wood and stone
carving, furniture. These crafts have been, and in some
cases still are, practised with such a degree of imagination,

29

such skill and insight, as to make their products works of art in every sense of the term. Benvenuto Cellini was a gold-smith and jeweller before he became a sculptor; in fact it was the common practice during the Renaissance period to apprentice a boy to a goldsmith as the preliminary step to his becoming a painter, sculptor, or architect. The status of the artist in times past was much nearer that of the arti-san than it is to-day or has been for a century and a half or more. The architect of ancient times was a sort of master builder and was often sculptor as well. The sculptor fre-quently undertook important works of construction, as wit-ness Phidias, who, besides executing a great deal of the sculpture himself, directed for Pericles all of the work of the architects, painters, and sculptors engaged upon the new buildings on the Athenian Acropolis after the Persians had destroyed the earlier temples. Of the position of the painter in Greece we have little to guide us, but we may judge from the respect with which the works of such men as Apelles and Zeuxis are mentioned that they enjoyed a high measure of consideration. The art of making and painting vases was much esteemed, and the craftsman signed his vase as the painter signs his canvas to-day.

The identity of the artist was lost, in Assyria and Baby-lonia, in that of the King, who claimed the credit for every-thing; and in Egypt, in the priesthood which held a mo-nopoly of all intellectual activity; and after the Alexandrian Age, for seven or eight centuries from about 300 B. C., the world was so busy being conquered and reorganized by the Romans, and then in being overrun by the Barbarians, that all record of the identity of the artist with his work was lost. Yet, during the Roman domination some of the most stu-pendous architectural monuments the world has seen were built—by whom? And the gardens and villas of the Roman patricians were crowded with thousands of statues by sculptors now unknown, unhonored, and unsung. Then for ages of darkness the civilized Western world was recovering from the blows rained upon its weakened body by the barbarian hordes, and the artist as an individual does not emerge until the Renaissance. During the Middle Ages—the three or four centuries between the close of the Dark Ages at about 1000 A. D. and the dawn of the Renaissance—his identity was merged in the guilds, associations, or unions, of workmen; masons, carvers, carpenters, painters; sometimes stationary in towns, sometimes so organized as to travel from place to place wherever their work was wanted. It was such bands of workmen who built the great cathedrals of France and England, who carved the statuary of the portals and decorated the interiors with vivid color.

When man's intellect began to awaken, to shake off the domination of the Church and think for itself, and men began to regard themselves as men, rather than as worms of the earth, we find individuality develop like a gourd-vine; and in this new atmosphere we discern the dim forms of Cimabue and Pisano, their contemporaries and immediate successors; the identity of the artist has once more emerged, never again to be lost so long as the printed word shall endure. The artist of the Renaissance did not have a studio in the accepted modern sense—he had a workshop, his *bottega*, which was also a salesroom. Here he made and sold his wares, and here he often lived and his apprentices with him. He would paint you an altar-piece and design and carve and gild and paint the frame, and deliver it at your house or parish church just as you pleased; or make a wedding-chest, to hold your linen or the hangings of your rooms, and paint and carve and gild that. He was architect, sculptor, painter, goldsmith, craftsman, contractor, shopman, all at once, or separately, as the occasion demanded. Giotto, a great painter, designed and built the Campanile or bell-tower of the Cathedral of Florence, and carved some of the statues that adorn it. The narrow specialism of the present day was unknown. The importance of the artist in the social scale and the body politic is indicated by his position below the *Arte*, or seven principal guilds, of Florence, ranked thus: notaries, dressers of cloth, changers, wool merchants, physicians, silk merchants, and skin merchants. It is evident that he could give himself few airs, in the early years of the Renaissance at least—although later he won for himself a far more important position, and became the confidant and intimate of statesmen and kings, like the Flemish painter, Peter Paul Rubens, who was ambassador to Spain and lived like a prince.

As time went on specialism gradually became the vogue and less and less did men practise more than one art. Social conditions so developed that an artist depended upon the patronage of a king or of some nobleman; the fulsome dedications of books and prints characteristic of the seventeenth and eighteenth centuries indicate a servility on the part of the artist repugnant to the spirit of to-day. It is only within the past century or so that the artist has shaken off this condition of servitude to a single patron and offered his work to the world at large.

The attitude of the artist toward his work has always been essentially simple. Your true artist looks upon his work as his daily job, like a man, as he should. The tiresome pose, the unspeakable twaddle current about art and artists, are in part an inheritance from the long-haired, romantic, Byronic era; partly the result of the airs of mystery second- and third- and tenth-rate artists have tried to surround themselves with, partly a product of the glamour with which the idea of a studio, where mysterious rites are supposed to be performed, is invested by some minds; the studios of figure painters, too, are filled with all sorts of plunder—stuffs, draperies, weapons, vases, all sorts of things the painter uses in his work and likes to have about him—creating a special kind of atmosphere. We have also to count with the imaginative layman who insists upon interpreting the artist's work for him, reading into it meanings the artist never dreamed of giving it. The artist is primarily absorbed in making something beautiful, or in working out some problem connected with that aim; if his trade is not in words he is usually inarticulate in direct ratio to his artistic ability. Then too, the painter works alone, shut up by himself because he does not wish to be disturbed—and the inveterate gusher bleats about "the master," withdrawn within himself, communing with his dreams. Whatever "the master" may feel in his inmost soul about his dreams, his aspirations, he keeps to himself, and only permits the world to guess at from the indications of his art. Enough has been said to suggest the ways in which an unhealthy impression has grown up.

The sculptor's studio is a workshop where a good deal of rough work is done with clay and plaster, and where there is apt to be an assistant or two about. And the architect's "studio" is no studio at all, but an office, where a great deal of mere business is transacted and where, at busy times, many draughtsmen, engineers, and office assistants are employed, and where art may very easily be crowded out by the pressure of business matters. Future chapters are devoted to the manner in which the architect, the sculptor, and the painter do their work, and the materials, appliances, and processes they use; but before we go into such technical details, we must have some notion of those physical limitations which restrict the means of expression proper to each of the three arts within pretty well defined bounds; the mode of expression in each art is subject to immense variation according to the taste, temperament, and training of the artist.

CHAPTER IV

THE MEANS OF EXPRESSION IN ARCHITECTURE, SCULPTURE, AND PAINTING

Architecture as the Envelope of Daily Life — Principles and Limitations of Architectural Design — Structural Necessities — Building Materials, their Qualities and Treatment — The Relation of Sculpture to Architecture and Painting — Architectonic Character — Action and Repose — Sculptural Light and Shade — Bas-relief — Materials for Sculpture — The Polychrome Treatment of Sculpture and of Architecture — Primitive Painting — Greek Use of Color — Drawing — Perspective — Light and Shade in Painting, or Chiaroscuro — Painting, a Translation of Nature — Special Characteristics of Painting — Easel Painting and Mural Painting — Their Fields and Functions — The Same Principles and Qualities Common to the Three Arts.

WHEN a man has protected his body against heat or cold with clothing, has provided for a supply of food, has invented ways to transport himself or his goods from place to place, to communicate with his fellow-men by speech or by the written or printed word, to ease their spiritual or cure their bodily ills, or to regularize their quarrels by process of law, there is still left in the world a vast plexus of industries directly related to Architecture; for the art of building is inclusive of those numberless trades, crafts, arts, and occupations, that complete the roll of man's activities.

Architecture is so close to us, is so much a part of our every-day life that we, most of us, grow to be quite unconscious of it, take it as a matter of course. We rise up from our beds in it, we break our fast in it, we leave it to go to our work only to pass through streets created by it and framed in it, and we return to it again at night; we repeat this round, day by day, and year by year, and scarcely see it. Surrounded on every hand by miracles of constructive genius, by the ugly and the beautiful, we are, with few exceptions, insensible to them. We are conscious perhaps of an especially tall building, or of a particularly big building, but they move us to no special wonder—wonder, in the sense that we should like to know how they came to be there; wonder, that they are the product of the human imagination. Of all the arts of man none so completely reflects his peculiar genius, nor should so influence the race, as that by which he houses himself or commemorates his civic or national importance. A building that has been lived in, worshipped in, has been the mute witness of human events trivial and great, seems to the sensitive observer to have acquired a soul. The successive tides of humanity lapping the base of a monument for ages leave their traces upon it, and something of the dignity, nobility, and pathos of their ebb and flow passes into it, for a lesson and a legacy to future generations of men.

Ignorance of the principles of architectural design, or of the processes of design, is no doubt responsible for the general purblindness; but the principles of design in Architecture are, as we have shown, the same as those in any other art; and there is no reason why a student of literature should not, if he has learned to analyze a work of literature and trace out its plan and superstructure, apply the same processes of analysis to a work of Architecture and come to a clear understanding of it, and a just estimate of its worth. Precisely as there are limitations which govern the expression of an idea in a novel and the use of the materials of a story, so there are limitations, and very stringent ones, in a piece of Architecture. The site; the aspect, whether sunny or the reverse; the use to which the structure is to be put; the number of stories required on a plot of a given size freely to permit the use desired; these are some of the elements which

A Pavilion of a TEMPLE AT PHILAE, now partially submerged by the Nile owing to the construction of the Assouan Dam. Chosen to show that the Egyptian style was susceptible of graceful and picturesque treatment. Besides the human figure, the Egyptians used the scarab, ibis, cat, serpent, hawk, and sun-disk, as sacred symbols, with lotus, reed, and papyrus forms ingeniously varied. Granite, porphyry, and basalt, difficult to work, imposed economy of labor, and simplicity of form resulted. Color was lavishly applied.

An ASSYRIAN BAS-RELIEF from the Palace of Asshur-nazir-pal, Nimrûd, representing the King attacking a city. The Assyrians covered their wall surfaces with painted sculpture or with colored tiles, frequently in designs which show that they were derived from the patterns of woven fabrics and hint therefore, with the character of their architecture, at the tent life of the nomadic tribes from which the people sprang. They brought this use of enamelled brick and tile to great perfection, using them to protect the sun-dried brick of the walls from the action of the weather. The architecture of Nineveh was influenced by the proximity of extensive stone quarries, while that of Babylon, situated in an alluvial plain, was built largely of brick and wood.

determine width and height, and the relation of the size of window openings to area of wall surface. These voids of the openings and these solids of wall surface are two of the most important means of architectural expression. A building may be made expressive of its purposes and use, even eloquent, by the mere disposition of the openings in the walls, without a column, without a moulding, without an ornament. Mass and proportion, heights and widths, walls and openings, mouldings and ornament, are the simple elements of the language of Architecture, capable of infinite modulation and variety, plastic to the expression of an individual temperament or of the genius of a nation. We must add to the limitations of use the limitations of structural necessities; the enormously thick walls required for a very tall structure would so cut down the floor area as to limit automatically the heights of buildings unless steel is used for vertical supports; the physical limitations imposed by materials upon great spans automatically limit the size of covered spaces unless steel is used to span them; the use of steel for such purposes is a development of the present generation. We have become accustomed to regard a building in which the old principles of masonry construction with heavy walls are followed, as the "monumental" type, and suitable for important public buildings; although steel is freely used in these also for many purposes, it is associated at present chiefly with commercial structures of considerable height; and our modern cities in America are becoming picturesque in consequence on a colossal and stupendous scale. We have not yet worked out a solution of some of the problems in our commercial buildings that satisfies the eye, and, through the eye, the judgment; the demand of the shopkeeper for the utmost possible area of show-window has resulted all too often in a building supported to all appearance, in the first story or so, entirely upon plate glass; and the judgment, through the eye, rejects the solution as unsatisfactory. For a sense of structural stability, without an appeal to a belief in the supernatural, is essential to a satisfactory architectural design. When we evidently have great weights to support, the eye and the mind demand adequate visible supports for these great weights. We find this principle observed in all the great buildings of the past.

Then we must reckon with the possibilities and limitations of brick and terra-cotta, stone and marble, their durability, color, texture, and suitability for the structure in question. Each of these has qualities peculiar to it and a treatment proper to each. Moreover, the use of one or the other establishes at once a certain range of possibilities of treatment for the building as a whole which must be respected under peril of failure.

We have thus indicated that in Architecture we are dealing with three dimensions, with ponderable masses—rough and heavy materials like stone and steel and brick—which must be wrought into a thing of beauty and utility, and that this is done by so disposing weights and supports, voids and solids, light-and-shade-producing elements like mouldings and ornament, as to give good proportion of mass to mass, of openings to walls, of openings to other openings, of solids to other solids, of light to shade, of interior spaces to other interior spaces; to give Harmony, Rhythm, Balance; to express the individual style of the designer, and to create the type of building proper to its destined use under given conditions of light in a given climate.

In Sculpture, also, we deal with ponderable substance; with three dimensions; with mass; with the play of light and shade which modulates the forms and the transitions from form to form; with an actual rather than an apparent

Balance, such as the way a statue stands well poised on its feet; with Rhythm, Harmony, always a general Design, and Beauty. In many of its qualities it is closely allied with Architecture, and in some with Painting. It is always a nice question how far a sculptor may go in the direction of a treatment of form by which light and shade are handled in a measurable degree as in Painting. It may be answered, I think, by the statement that the more closely a piece of Sculpture is related to a work of Architecture, the more it must partake of the qualities of Architecture, have more repose, be modelled in well-marked planes, be less realistic; be, in short, architectonic; the isolated group or figure with nothing architectural near it except the pedestal, which is in this case subordinate to the Sculpture, may very properly on the other hand approach reality, be accorded a much freer treatment and a modulation of form that will cause the light and shade to interfuse somewhat as in Painting. One law would seem to have been very definitely established in the long history of Sculpture—the necessity for Repose; violent or arrested action is never to be found in the greatest work; the repose may be absolute, or the figure may seem to be quivering into action, or to have just that moment reached repose; the sculptor of judgment and taste selects the instant when every line, every form, is in one of those exquisite states of equilibrium. There is in Sculpture nothing more tiresome than arrested action, or over-dramatic action. We have all seen the statue of the orator, hand in breast, one arm extended in menace or exhortation, and subconsciously wished that he would put it down and rest. On the other hand, we have seen figures rigid as stakes, which look not only as though they never had moved, but never could. On the Pincian Hill, in Rome, there is a modern group representing two brothers, one prostrate and presumably wounded, the other standing astride his brother's body in a dramatic attitude of defense and defiance; it is not a sculptural conception; the sculptor did not choose the moment in the story that would have made it possible for him to create a great piece of Sculpture; the moment he chose was one that might conceivably have been successfully treated in Painting. I would not be understood as saying that Sculpture must not be dramatic—far from it. But the sculptor must know how to dramatize the moment or the story. Nothing could be more dramatic, more poignant, more moving in its repose, than Rodin's group representing the despairing, starved-out Burghers of Calais delivering up the keys of their beleaguered city.

In good Sculpture one is not conscious of arms and legs, because they are arranged in such a way that they contribute to a sense of Balance, Rhythm, Unity, and Repose; especially Unity, for nothing cuts up a group of figures into an agglomeration of unrelated parts so much as the liney, leggy appearance an unskilful use or treatment of the limbs creates. Good Sculpture also avoids the use of intensely dark shadows for accents—technically called blacks—because such blacks cut up a figure or a group and destroy the sense of Unity; it also avoids "holes" or spaces between forms through which we may see beyond the group or figure; this requires much study, skill, and resourcefulness, for most Sculpture is to be seen from every side and from an infinite number of points of view, far off or close by, higher or lower, and yet from every conceivable view-point it must always be agreeable if it cannot always be beautiful. The competent sculptor, therefore, arranges the arms and legs, the drapery and other adjuncts, to avoid holes and make the elements of his design fall into agreeable relations.

Up to this point we have been discussing Sculpture "in

the round" or fully detached. A word as to Sculpture in high relief but attached to a background, *alto relievo*, and Sculpture in low relief, *basso relievo*, or bas-relief. In these forms of Sculpture the degree of relief governs the appropriate treatment of the forms; the closer it approaches low relief, the more it must be treated in planes; and the lower the relief, the more closely it approximates the effect of a drawing, the forms being so treated that they cast shadows, or receive the light, or modulate the shade, as these would appear in a flat drawing. Drawing is a term constantly used in discussing Sculpture; good drawing, that is, a fine sense of line and light-and-shade, is an inseparable property of good Sculpture.

The materials used for Sculpture are various; each has its appropriate treatment, and each, as in Architecture, imposes a definite character upon the work. Basalt, granite, marble, limestone, sandstone, bronze, terra-cotta, and wood, are all materials in which great Sculpture has been wrought. Much Egyptian sculpture was done in granite and basalt, both of them extremely hard, especially basalt, which is so difficult to cut that the utmost simplicity of form was necessary to avoid untold labor; a source of that wonderful simplification and unity found in so much Egyptian work. Upon the other hand, there are Egyptian carvings in fine-grained sandstone that are like jewelry in their exquisite refinement and elaboration of detail. Marble has always been a favored material for Sculpture, is far more tractable than granite, easily worked, and has a crystalline structure which permits the light to penetrate somewhat below the surface and make it translucent. The treatment proper for marble is simpler than that for bronze, wherein a greater degree of elaboration of detail is permissible. Terra-cotta, also, cast in clay from the plaster casts of the sculptor's clay model or modelled directly in terra-cotta clay, and baked, is susceptible of great freedom of treatment; while wood has its own technical limitations and resources, due to its color, grain, and tendency to split.

Modern Sculpture has denied itself a resource of effect in the use of color of which the sculptor of the past made superb use. The earliest Greek sculptural forms were painted, and they were modelled in such a way as to prepare for the addition of color to fully express them. At the height of Grecian culture there were numbers of chryselephantine statues, consisting of plates of ivory, bent or shaped over a wooden or clay form, to represent the flesh, and plates of gold wrought into the folds of the drapery by bending or beating or casting; with laudable thrift the gold was made removable so that in time of national stress it might be converted into currency. The eyes were undoubtedly colored, sometimes set with sapphires; and the most famous one, the statue of Athene Parthenos, the tutelary goddess of Athens, in the Parthenon on the Acropolis, wore an actual cloak or peplum, woven by the women of Athens; the subject of the Frieze of the Parthenon is the procession in which this peplum was carried from the city and solemnly presented to the goddess. Egyptian and Assyrian Sculpture was brilliantly colored. Much of the sculpture of the Middle Ages was polychromatic, particularly that destined for the interior of buildings; and in the Renaissance terra-cottas of the Della Robbia family, the color was applied as glazes. Chinese and Japanese sculptors have ever delighted in the use of glazed porcelain and earthenware, in lacquers and gilding upon wood, and in patines on bronze of various colors. A revival of the use of color in Sculpture is much to be desired. Some sculptors believe that no actual pigment or glaze should be used, but that color should be suggested

44

by textures, by the treatment of surfaces, by light and shade. There is no question but that in unskilful hands many horrors might be added to the sum of those already in the world; but handled with tact and discretion, and with a sense of the proper conventional coloration to adopt, the addition of color to form is very beautiful. Sculpture to-day frequently repels the average person because mere form, in the absence of the technical knowledge to appreciate it, and divested of its familiar color, seems cold and lifeless.

Sculpture, then, has plastic form, mass, light and shade, and color, at its command, as means of expression of the thought that lies behind it.

Architecture, too, may avail itself of the resources of color in several ways: in mural or wall painting and decoration; in mosaic work, a design or picture executed in small cubes or tesseræ of marble, glass, or tile; in colored terracotta or faience; in stained and painted glass in windows; and in the use of colored Sculpture. It is to be observed that the kind of color, the choice of colors, tones, or tints, to be used in the enhancement of either Architecture or Sculpture are precisely similar in principle; the color must not be naturalistic, must not simulate that of natural objects. It must be in practically flat tones. The colored forms must be highly conventionalized; that is to say, simplified, and made to count as Pattern. This applies to all forms, human, animal, or vegetable. Precisely as Sculpture must take on architectonic character as it becomes intimately related to a building, so must colored decoration, whether painted with pigments, made up of colored tesseræ as in mosaic, applied in glazes as in tile or terra-cotta, or used as colored light as in stained glass.

In Painting, we do not deal with bulk, with the three dimensions of height, width, and thickness, in the same sense that we do in Architecture and Sculpture. Painting represents bulk and indicates the third dimension upon a flat surface having only two dimensions, namely: height and width. Primitive painting, as a general rule—in which we will, for the sake of simplicity, include drawing—owing to lack of skill, took little account of the third dimension, or attempted its representation in crude, and what now seem to us to be amusing, ways. Greek vase painting is merely flat drawing in one or two colors. But, judging from the stories told of the work of Apelles and Zeuxis, Greek painting other than vase-painting was far advanced toward realism, a representation of natural objects to simulate reality by the use of natural colors; but nothing has survived to us of the great masters. We may only believe that a race as sensitive to beauty of line and mass and to the most subtle refinements of light and shade as the Greeks, must have had a color sense. The tender color of the little figurines dug up at Tanagra in Bœotia, and in some parts of Attica, indicate that Greek color was not as barbarically crude as some archæologists would lead us to think. Greek buildings were undoubtedly colored, but they could not have been as ugly as some modern restorations represent. I believe that the Greeks and the Egyptians had discovered the secret of broken color—the juxtaposition of small areas of two pure colors side by side to produce the effect of a third, as: red and blue to produce a purple or violet.

It is evident that the means and modes of expression in Painting must differ radically from those proper to Architecture and Sculpture. These may borrow one or two of the elements which go to make up the art of Painting, such as Color and Drawing. But Painting, in order to give the impression of relief, of depth, which Architecture and Sculpture possess in their own nature, makes use of a tributary science, that of Perspective, by means of which any object, or any scene, may be portrayed in correct relation to other objects, in size or shape, from a fixed or assumed point of view. Upon analysis it is found that straight lines converge to one or more points, called vanishing-points; these points are in a line, the horizon line, coincident with a horizontal plane passing through the eye of the observer whether he is lying down in a valley, or erect upon the summit of a mountain. The simplest illustration of this simple law is a straight railroad track on a plain of considerable extent. Standing midway of the rails they seem to meet at a point opposite the eyes; upon slowly bending the knees, this point will be seen to lower with the eyes; climbing a box, or a stepladder, this point opposite the eyes, the vanishing-point, climbs with us. If we move from between the tracks toward the left, the two rails will pass from our right side and meet as before, at the height of the eyes, to the left of the track; and if we move to the right, then the rails will run from our left to our right. This principle is applied to any object or group of objects of any shape or size; for instance, indoors, to every object in the room: chairs, tables, boxes, books, vases, everything. And to everything out of doors also. When many objects stand at all sorts of angles to each other, they will all have their own vanishing-points, but the vanishing-points of all of them will be in one horizontal plane at the height of the eye, wherever the eye is, or is assumed to be. If one person is seated, and another is standing directly behind him, and both draw the same object, say a table, the representation of the object in their respective drawings will be different in each, because the person standing up has a higher horizon line than the one sitting down. And if they draw more than one object from their respective points of view, the relations of these objects and their apparent shapes in the drawings will be different. The person standing up may be able to see something on the other side of the table which the table hides from the seated one. Architecture and Sculpture do not have to borrow this science to produce the effect of the third dimension, because they possess all three dimensions in themselves. But they both make allowance for its laws—as to which let two simple illustrations suffice: roofs apparently flatten out when seen in perspective, and to make them appear of the desired height in relation to the rest of the building, they have to be built much higher to allow for this apparent flattening; a statue to be seen from below must have a neck longer than nature, or the head will seem to be sunken between the shoulders.

The science of Perspective was no doubt known to the Greeks, in some of its simpler aspects; they used it to a limited extent; and it was known to the decorative painters of Græco-Roman times, as the wall paintings of Pompeii testify. But with much else it lapsed, was forgotten, and then was rediscovered in the days of the Renaissance. Before that, and perhaps leading to it, the secrets of light and shade had been discovered—*chiaroscuro*, as the Italians called it, from *chiaro*, light, *oscuro*, dark.

Up to the time of Cimabue, painting had been flat colored drawing, done by formulas handed down in the painters' guilds, or from father to son; he first dared to look at nature and follow her—very timidly to be sure—but he broke the ground and sowed the seed. Giotto, following immediately after, went farther, although his work looks flat enough to us moderns; and from the work of these pioneers to the last refinements of the present, is one steady progression in the discovery of the resources of Painting, and the use of its elements of light and shade, color, and perspective.

MURAL PAINTING in the Auditorium of the Sorbonne, the University of Paris, by PIERRE-CÉCILE PUVIS DE CHAVANNES, the most important work of this modern master, born 1824 at Lyons, died at Paris 1898. A grey-green landscape, a yellow sky, figures robed in soft tones of blue, white, violet, and cool red, the picture breathes the peace of that intellectual sphere where reason reigns and the stress of a world of noisy and futile striving after material things is forgotten.

DIAGRAM BY BEN J. LUBSCHEZ illustrating some of the principles of PERSPECTIVE. Parallel horizontal lines are prolonged to show that they meet in a Vanishing-Point on the Horizon Line which is at the level of the Station-Point, viz.: the eye of the observer or the lens of the camera. The distance between the images of the lamp-posts diminishes as these recede into the distance. The height of the Horizon Line varies with that of the Station-Point.

With drawing, color, perspective, and light and shade, the painter is equipped to express anything that may be expressed in Painting, from the most sublime vision to the most trivial incident of daily life, from dawn to dawn again.

These are the means, the things Architecture, Painting, and Sculpture are done with. The modes, the way these things are used, are many.

One principle is universally recognized now—that Painting is a kind of translation of the appearance of an object or of a scene, a representation, not imitation. The man who paints a dollar-bill so that it might deceive a bank teller has wasted his time. As a work of art his imitation is worthless. As currency it is useless. To paint a tree with every leaf accounted for as far as may be humanly possible is not to paint the tree but the leaves. To show every hair upon a person's head is not to paint his hair but his hairs. More and more, as the laws of light and of color are better understood, it is seen that a truthful rendition of a subject is a rendition of that subject as seen in a given light at a given moment, and that the truth is therefore purely relative. An object fully and brightly lighted has not at all the same appearance, even may not seem to be the same shape, and certainly has not the same color, as the same object seen in deep shadow. As a matter of fact, when one looks at a tree, or the hair on a man's head, one sees, not the leaves and not the hairs, but the play of light and shade on masses of leaves and masses of hair; and by painting this play of light and shade and the way it modifies the actual color of the subject—which is called its local color—one paints the subject.

In a painting, besides the general characteristics of all works of art, Design, Proportion, Balance, Rhythm, Pattern, and so on, we have to reckon with others, applicable, like Perspective, especially to itself, such as Tone, Color,

Value, Key or Pitch, Vibration, Atmosphere, Envelope. Denman Ross defines Color as the Quality of light in a Tone, and Value as the Amount of light in a Tone. Key, or Pitch, is applicable to the picture as a whole: when there is much light the Key or Pitch is high, and vice versa. Vibration is that quality in a painting which makes the light seem to shimmer and the air to be full of dancing motes. Atmosphere and Envelope are interchangeable terms; when there seems to be air in the picture, that is Atmosphere; when forms are bathed in Atmosphere they are said to have an Envelope, or to be Enveloped.

Not all of these are availed of in all kinds of painting. Modern paintings are broadly divisible into two general classes, Easel Pictures and Mural Paintings. By an easel picture is meant a picture of a size that may be painted upon a painter's easel, and be easily transported from place to place and hung up anywhere; and by association and inference is assumed to deal with the natural aspects of things or of human beings; portraits, landscapes, still life, *genre* —meaning paintings illustrative of the homely incidents of every-day life—are all, if portable, in the category of easel pictures. A mural painting, on the other hand, is intended to be permanently fixed on a wall, is sometimes painted directly upon the wall; ceiling paintings are included in this category, but are susceptible of a more airy and atmospheric treatment, due to their position and the very necessary avoidance of any appearance of heaviness.

The aims in a Mural Painting are quite distinct from those in an easel picture. The easel picture deals primarily with the actual, the Mural Painting with the ideal. It will be recalled that the moment Painting and Sculpture come into close relation with Architecture their nature changes, and they must be treated in a conventional—in the sense of conventionalized—architectonic, manner. In an easel picture one seems to be looking through the frame, as through a window, into a space which the painter has filled with figures or landscape, with light or with gloom. Whatever other qualities a Mural Painting may possess, it fails of being a true one if it seems to pierce an opening in the wall through which one may look into a space beyond the plane of the wall. The Plane of the Wall, the feeling that the painting is painted on the very wall, must be preserved. The ways in which the solution of this problem have been managed will be treated of in the chapter dealing with the Technique of Painting. Suffice it to say here, discussing as we are only the means and modes of expression in a general sense, that Mural Painting dispenses with Envelope or Atmosphere, and, so far as Vibration relates to Atmosphere, dispenses with that also. Drawing and Pattern are of paramount importance, and the greater of these is Pattern. A mural decoration will be agreeable if the Pattern is good, although the Drawing may be bad. Good Color is of course an element of good Pattern; the best of Patterns may be destroyed by offensive and discordant color elements.

There is no place in Mural Painting for the melting lights and shadows such as we see for example in the work of Murillo. The aim of realistic painting is to destroy the sense of the surface upon which the painting is made, in order to create an illusion of depth, roundness, relief, an approximation of reality. Such effects are alien to the nature and aim of Mural Painting. The primary purpose of a mural painting is to decorate a given space or surface; but it has another function—to record the events of history, the progress of the human mind and spirit, and so to teach and to elevate the human soul. In this function mural work has a literary content or meaning; and all too often the meaning, the story-telling quality, is given precedence over those essential qualities lacking which it is not worth the doing—Design, Pattern, Color.

The expression of individuality or of emotion by the play of feature, is of questionable propriety here, where all the elements are to be so disposed and arranged as to direct the emotion or the thought of the observer in a certain desired direction. To take an extreme example for the sake of illustration: if, in a Mural Painting, a man were to be seen escaping from a bear, the expression of his face would count for very little at a distance, but the expression of the action of his body would be very important and the speed of fear should be instinct in every line of it. Of course, unless this act of escape from the bear contributed in an absolutely direct and positive manner toward the meaning of the picture as a whole, it would be irrelevant and disturbing. And if, for another example, an individual is seen welcoming other persons, his whole attitude must be one of welcome that may be seen and understood from a long distance, a distance at which a sweet smile would be quite indistinguishable.

I am trying to state the proposition that in a Mural Painting there must be a large general idea that must be conveyed to the observer by large means, and that all trivialities of gesture or expression, everything irrelevant to the large general idea, must be suppressed.

We have thus seen that, while in Architecture, Sculpture, and Painting, the materials, means, and modes of expression appropriate to each vary widely, the same principles and qualities are common to all—and this cannot be too often repeated nor too strongly emphasized. Design, Proportion, Balance or Symmetry, Rhythm, Pattern, Harmony, Contrast, Style, link them in an essential unity.

CHAPTER V

THE TECHNIQUE OF ARCHITECTURE

What Technique Is — The Education of the Architect — His Office and His
Staff — The Development of Sketches, Working Drawings, and Detail
Drawings — Specifications — Administration and Supervision — Color
and Furnishings — Landscape Work — The Execution of a Vision.

AN intelligent appreciation of a work of art in any kind
presupposes some knowledge of the processes by which it
was brought into being. Those processes are not miracles,
even though the building, the picture, the symphony, the
statue, should seem to have been miraculously created, so
beautiful it is, so hidden the means. I will give as clear an
idea as I can of the steps an artist follows in the conception and completion of a work of Architecture, of Sculpture,
or of Painting. The practice of every individual varies;
therefore it is only possible to state those general methods
most men follow, and it is necessary to omit, for the general
reader, many of those more recondite points of technique
that would be of interest only to one who is intending the
practice of an art.

At the outset we must define this word, Technique, heard
so frequently as part of the jargon of art. It simply means
the way in which a thing is done. There is a general way
to paint a picture which may be described as the Technique
of Painting; every painter has his own way of going about
it, and so we speak of his technique, of the breadth of his
technique—meaning a free, broad handling of his pigments,
color masses, light and shade—or of his dry, or tight, technique, qualities the reverse of free and broad. Of the sculptor
and his work, for dry or tight would be substituted such
terms as hard or tinny. In the case of the architect we must

distinguish between the means and the result, the means being the drawings and the result the building; the term technique is applicable to his drawings, which would be qualified or described as the painter's drawings or paintings are described; we speak of the architect's executed work as big in feeling, or as broken up, or fussy; we call the building dry if it lacks richness of form or light and shade; but we seldom refer to the architect's technique and we call his designs by a host of names which, as the slang of the office or the atelier, need not concern us here.

The technique of architectural drawing and of general office and drafting-room practice is not of special interest to the layman, although architectural draftsmanship is an exquisite and difficult craft. Suffice it to say here that an architect's drawings are made on various kinds of paper, in pencil, ink, and water-color. Free-hand sketches are made in black-and-white, or water-color or pastel. By black-and-white is meant a drawing in various shades of black, gray, and white, whether produced by pencil, pen and ink, or brush work.

Before we tell how an architect does his work, let us understand how he becomes an architect. He either attends a course in architecture at some technical school, a college, or university, and receives a degree or not as the case may be; or he enters the office of a practising architect, sometimes as a boy of high-school age or younger, sometimes after the usual college or university education; before he enters practice on his own account he should have, and frequently does have, a trip abroad for sketching and study of the architecture of the Old World, that he may see how the masters of the craft have solved the thousands of problems that will sooner or later confront him; not that he may copy these solutions, but that he may master the underlying

THE PARTHENON at Athens, built by the architects ICTINUS and CALLICRATES between 454 and 438 B. C. and dedicated to the virgin Athena. It was embellished with the sculpture of PHIDIAS and decorated without and within with color. In it culminates the development of the Doric mode through a long series of temples, and replaces that burnt by the Persians in 480 B. C. Used by the Turks as a powder magazine, it was almost destroyed by an explosion caused by a Venetian shell.

The TEMPLE OF CONCORD at Agrigentum (the modern Girgenti), in Sicily; one of the early temples in the Doric style, erected in an important Greek colony. A comparison of the column capitals and the entablature above them with those of the Parthenon indicates the refinement the Doric order experienced in a century, this structure having been built by an unknown architect about 550 B. C., of a coarse-grained stone covered with a thin coat of fine hard stucco plaster.

principles which led to them. Sometimes he enters such schools as the School of Fine Arts in Paris, the *École des Beaux-Arts*, which has been so generously hospitable to foreign students.

An architect's office is in many ways like any business office, but with a drafting-room, where the drawings are made, as the important unit. There may be a large and complex, or a small and simple staff of assistants, controlled and directed by the architect to carry out his conceptions. Frequently he has a partner or partners to relieve him of the details of administration, or to supplement or complement his own talents.

The first step toward the creation of a building is an interview with the client, who describes his needs. The client may be a private person or a building committee. The architect takes notes of the requirements and makes a little free-hand sketch of the plan, the elevation—a front of the building—and a section, which is like a slice through the building showing the interior. From these are elaborated more careful sketches drawn to scale—that is, at a size in which a fraction of an inch on the drawing represents a foot in the future building; these are revised in consultation with the client until all the general dispositions of the rooms, doors, windows, staircases, elevators, and the like, in plan, and the general character of the exterior and of the principal rooms, are tentatively established.

The next step is the Working Drawings, which are accurate geometrical drawings in line, which show only two dimensions on each drawing—in a plan, length and width are shown; the elevations and sections show the third dimension, the height, with one of the others, either length or width. By a convention the eye is assumed to be exactly opposite every point in the object drawn, so that every part of it may be exactly measured. All relations of Scale, Balance, Pattern, Rhythm, and Proportion are established by these drawings, which are made, when finally developed, on transparent tracing-paper or linen, from which duplicates are made, by the action of light on sensitized paper, for the use of the builder. These blue prints are often spoken of by the innocent as though they were the original rather than the by-product; current fiction teems with scenes in which the sunburned hero and the blue print play rôles of almost equal importance. These Working Drawings show all the items of construction of the building; during the course of assembling, arranging, and adjusting all this vast mass of information and putting it down on paper in a clear and understandable form, the idea contained in the preliminary studies, or sketches, receives many modifications to make it workable and buildable and to refine and perfect every proportion of the exterior and interior.

Accompanying these Working Drawings are the Specifications, which constitute a written description of all the materials to be used in the structure in minute detail, with directions to the workmen as to how the work is to be done. When the Working Drawings and Specifications are finished they are issued to builders for estimates of the cost. A Contract is then entered into for the construction of the building. The architect draws up this Contract, of which the Working Drawings and Specifications form a part.

The architect then proceeds to make Detail Drawings. In a properly designed building by a conscientious architect there is not a detail the eye may fall upon that has not been carefully studied, practically and æsthetically, and a drawing, sometimes several, made of it. While the building is proceeding there are frequent visits by the architect or his deputy to see that the work is being executed in accordance with the drawings and specifications; also to modelling shops where the ornamental work of stone, plaster, wood, or metal is being modelled and to distant quarries, kilns, and mills where work is being fabricated.

Throughout there has been a probably voluminous correspondence between the architect's office, the client, and the contractors, and numberless interviews with them and with the manufacturers of all the thousand and one materials and appliances which enter into the construction of a modern building. Besides this, if the building has any pretensions to importance, the architect has been in consultation with painters and sculptors, determining the character and scale of mural paintings and sculpture, and the colors and finishes of walls, ceilings, and woodwork. A building, however beautiful in itself, is not usable without furniture, and its beauty is impaired unless the furniture, which includes hangings, lighting fixtures, rugs or other floor coverings, is not only beautiful itself, but harmonious with its setting, the building, and the several units harmonious with each other. The average house or building furnished by the client looks, to the practised eye, very much as a fugue of Bach would sound if it were performed with "variations by the band-master." The simile of a fugue is excellent in connection with a work of architecture, for, in both, voices enter one by one into the composition and are woven into an intricate web of beauty to which nothing more can be added and from which nothing can be subtracted without mutilating the fabric. Architecture was once described as frozen music, and the world has gone on repeating the phrase like Pretty Poll; architecture is no more frozen music than it is frozen mud; there is nothing frozen about good architecture; it is warm and human, full of the movement that is Rhythm, full of color and springing life.

The building designed, there remains another function of the well-rounded architect—the landscape work. Trained as he is in the disposition of forms and of masses of color, to that supersense of the third dimension by which he imagines himself as being actually within the picture he is creating, walking about in it and seeing it from a thousand changing points of view, he is usually qualified to carry out what he had conceived to be the appropriate and beautiful setting for the building he has designed. This work entails a series of steps similar to those in the creation of the building itself.

This is a mere outline, a sketch, of what is done, with many details omitted. And one may well wonder how it is possible to hold fast to the vision of the building as it first presented itself, how to get it executed by other hands, often by no means sympathetic and frequently unskilled, and how at last, in spite of the complexities, the distractions not merely of the business details of one commission, but of many, the months and years of work first in the office and then at the shops and in the building, and the interposition of so many personalities between the designer and his finished work, it is possible to have the building infused with the personality of the architect.

He is only enabled to hold his vision fresh and clear, and endure the long, slow processes, the endless delays, the terrible tedium of many of his duties, by what may be described as a kind of passion for the creation of beauty, and this sees him through. The training of the eye, the mind, the taste, and the constructive and executive faculties of the architect are never completed. It is one of the compensations of the laborious life of the conscientious artist that there is always something more to learn about form and color, light and shade, character and style.

CHAPTER VI

THE TECHNIQUE OF SCULPTURE

The Sculptor's Conception — His Materials and Tools — His First Sketch —
The Steps Following — Working by Planes and Working by Profiles —
Modelling a Head — Armatures and Pointing-up — Falsification of Fact
for Truth of Effect — Proper Treatment of Sculpture for Execution in
Various Materials — Carving a Statue — Bas-Relief — Medals and Coins —
The Education of the Sculptor — His Studio and Its Atmosphere.

UNLIKE the architect, neither the sculptor nor the painter
need wait for a commission before creating a composition,
unless he is an architectural sculptor only, or a mural painter
pure and simple. It has, I hope, been made clear in a preceding chapter that a mural painting or a piece of architectural sculpture must be conceived and executed with
reference to the exact place it is to occupy. The description
we are about to give of the technique of the sculptor applies
equally to free-standing sculpture or to architectural sculpture; the differences between these lie in character, not in
method.

The materials a sculptor uses are: wet clay; plasteline,
a composition which does not dry and crack and need not be
kept wet as clay must be; and prepared wax. An idea for
a figure or a group occurs to him; he sees it in his mind's
eye, more or less clearly, more or less vaguely, as the architect first sees his building, the painter his picture, the
musician his song, the poet his sonnet. It is as yet only an
intangible thought, still to be made visible to others. He
takes a lump of clay or plasteline and, with his fingers and his

63

tools—flattish wooden spatulas and wire loops of different shapes and sizes inserted in wooden handles—he models the plastic material into the general guise of his vision. The top of his modelling stand works on a pivot so that he may turn the figure around and view it in various lights from every possible point of view. This little sketch may be only four or five inches high, but, like the thumb-nail sketch of the architect, or the phrase of the musician, contains the germ of the completed work. The sculptor then enlarges this sketch to a size several times greater. For this larger sketch an armature is required. An armature is a sort of skeleton without ribs or head, but with arms, legs, spine, and neck, made of wire—hard lead, copper, or galvanized iron—bent into the general attitude and shape of the little sketch model. Without the armature the model would sag of its own weight as the human body would without its skeleton. The feet of the armature secured to the modelling stand, the sculptor proceeds to clothe this skeleton with clay or plasteline— wax is used chiefly for very small figures or for models of coins or medals—squeezing it around the wires and building out the forms of the body. When the general masses of the body, head, and limbs are approximately arrived at, he begins with fingers and tools to correct and modify the forms and establish their drawing and their planes. The profile of any form as seen in any position is, in Sculpture, the drawing of that form. Any surface, however rounded it may seem to be, may be resolved upon examination into a series of approximately flat planes. Taking the face as an illustration, we have the general plane of the forehead, the general planes of the cheeks, the general plane beneath the nose in which the mouth and chin lie. These are the big, main planes; and each is made up of other, minor planes and these again of lesser ones; and so of any part of the body. Some

The ATHENIAN ACROPOLIS from the northwest. In the foreground is the so-called Theseum, the best preserved Doric temple in Greece; although very small, like the Parthenon, visible on the Acropolis beyond, its scale is so perfect that it seems from some distance to be a large building. Vestiges of the polychrome treatment still remain. It is of the very best period of Athenian architecture, and exhibits one more optical refinement than the Parthenon; its authorship is uncertain.

The CHORAGIC MONUMENT OF LYSICRATES, built in Athens by an unknown artist in the reign of Alexander the Great. A bronze tripod, the prize at the Festival of Dionysus (Roman, Bacchus) stood upon the foliated marble finial.

THE STOOPING DISCOBOLUS, by MYRON, an Athenian sculptor born about 480 B. C. It exemplifies the perfection of action momentarily arrested; the downward sweep of body and arm is finished and is about to flow smoothly into the upward swing.

sculptors work by establishing the planes first; some by establishing the profiles of forms first and then connecting them with planes; as for example: in modelling a head, to build up the profile of the face and the top and back of the head exactly as it looks from the side; then the outline of the head and ears as it looks from straight in front; then the three-quarter views of the face and back of the head; then connecting these mere profiles with clay, and then establishing an infinite number of intermediate profiles or outlines in the order of their importance. By this method the absolute drawing of every mass, or contour of a mass or form, is definitely fixed. The other method, working by planes, is about like this: a mass of soft clay or plasteline— no armature is required if we are modelling a head—is thoroughly kneaded and pounded together, to fill up all possible voids, and then cut with wire tools into the approximate shape of the head. At this stage it looks something like the wooden heads in milliners' windows. Then the sculptor presses his thumbs on the places where the eyes will be and forms the plane of the eyes; changing the pressure out and down creates the cheek-bones; he returns to the nose and, using the thumb and forefinger as required, of both hands, he presses at each side of the nose-to-be, pressing out and down again to create the plane of the cheeks. Pressure under the nose develops the plane of the mouth and chin; under the jaw, the jaw-bone. A deft touch in the soft clay sketches in the eyelids, another, the lips. Long before this a face has seemed to smile through the clay as though it had always been there and the sculptor had but released it from its enveloping matrix. It is amazing how rapidly a skilful artist will thus create life out of dead earth. The sculptor then corrects profiles and planes and carries out the minor details and refinements of surface and expression. Many men have many methods, but these two are most easily describable.

Although we have described these as applied to the modelling of a head, the same principles apply to a whole figure. Sometimes, if the work is to be a statuette, the artist will go on refining the surfaces and profiles of the sketch to an exquisite degree of finish. But if a sketch for a life-size, or larger, figure is in question, he only carries it to a point where the character is clearly marked, the action expressed, the great masses of light and shade established, Balance and Rhythm secured. A cast is then made of the sketch model absolutely reproducing it in plaster of Paris, and which will therefore bear handling. The enlargement, or "pointing up" of the sketch to the size desired, is a mechanical matter and the first part of the process is turned over to men who make a business of it. Resort is had to a kind of gigantic pantograph; the distance between any two points on the small model is automatically increased by the machine to the size desired. An armature is made of strong iron pipe, bent and adjusted to follow the action of the figure, as shown by the sketch, and as the pantograph indicates it to be at the larger scale. The pieces of pipe for the arms and legs are often put together in such a way that they may be moved, in case the sculptor should feel a change desirable. This is clothed with clay by the fistful, pounded into a solid mass until it begins to resemble a human figure. The enlarging machine is so constructed that one leg will move in unison with the other, and a nail is driven into the clay of the enlarged model and left sticking out until its head just touches the tip of the enlarging leg; the head of this nail may give the position of the tip of the nose, or the point of the shoulder; this process repeated again and again all over the figure, it is soon bristling with nails, the head of each representing a certain point on the plaster sketch model, each of these points being marked on the latter with a lead-pencil. Clay is then built up around these nails flush with their heads, the nails pulled out, and the figure takes on the appearance of the forms of the sketch, but several times larger. It is of course unnecessary to enlarge every detail. The sculptor needs only the main planes and points, for, in enlarging a small model its defects and inaccuracies are magnified in proportion. Besides, the problem of treating a figure on a large scale is quite a different one from the treatment of a statuette; more detail is permissible, and yet the difficulty of indicating detail in a broad and convincing way is increased by the larger scale. So, having the main points accurately fixed, he begins afresh to study every plane, every profile, the flow of every line, how lines should be opposed or repeated by other lines, how the lights and shadows fall, from every conceivable point of view. Frequently, for the position the figure is to occupy, higher or lower as the case may be, distortion and falsification are required for truth of effect. Planes must be tipped forward or back, this way or that, the neck must be lengthened, things done to the eyes and nose and so on, in order that when placed in its destined position the figure shall look right. When it is thoroughly studied and carried as far as it can be in clay, a plaster cast is made of it and the sculptor then works over this plaster cast with the greatest care, scraping and smoothing and refining surfaces, giving them textures, and softening or sharpening details as he feels they require it, until it is as beautiful as he can make it. It is then ready to cast in bronze—a highly technical process and in modern times not a part of the sculptor's craft. Had the figure been destined for execution in marble or stone it would have been given another sort of treatment; the last finishing process on the large plaster model would be modified or omitted; but first, and most important, there are attitudes of the body for which marble is unsuited—a very simple example would be one in which a figure is drawn up to its full height with one arm extended straight out at a right angle with the body. Either this arm must be cut from a separate piece of marble and jointed on at the shoulder, or, for the sake of having the whole figure in one piece, an enormous block of marble must be provided and all of it beyond the body wasted for this arm. And whichever way it were done, there would be constant danger and likelihood that the arm would eventually crack and fall off or be broken off. This attitude, or almost any attitude, may however be perfectly and safely executed in bronze.

The limitations of the material therefore impose a definite character upon the work, and the sculptor with a grasp upon these limitations of his materials and upon his art, composes his figure or group with definite reference to the material in which it will be executed. If he were modelling for execution in faience—glazed earthenware—he would not only model all his forms much more crisply than usual to allow for the softening of edges and the filling up of hollows by the colored glazes, but he would so model them as to catch and hold the glaze where he wants accent or a richer coloration, and would make allowance throughout for the tendency the glaze has to run off the high places and gather in the hollows. This technique is very fascinating and one of which the Chinese and Japanese are masters.

Returning, after this digression, to execution in marble, the reader will no doubt recall many marble groups or figures in which the stump of a tree or something of that sort is placed beside a part of the figure, or under it—as under the belly of a prancing horse. These are cases wherein the limitations of the material were ignored or exceeded and resort was had to this expedient to carry the weight and make the figure stand up.

To reproduce the full-size plaster model in marble, the early part of the work is turned over to skilful carvers, who, taking the rough block of stone, rough out the figure by a series of careful measurements, and then as soon as points can be fixed for it, the pantograph is brought into play—or, rather, a modification of it, since the figure is not being enlarged. Three points are established, coinciding with the three legs of the machine, and a fourth is found on the plaster cast by a sliding and movable metal rod with a point. This point is made to touch a spot on the plaster cast, the rod secured with a set-screw, the point marked for identification with a lead-pencil, the machine transferred to the marble and the three legs placed on the three fixed points which agree with the three on the plaster. The marble is then cut away until the point of the metal rod when slid out to the same extent as on the plaster model exactly touches the marble. Of course, the principal points are always found first, and the marble cut away in planes, the larger at first and then the smaller ones, until the figure is almost like the original plaster. Both are covered by this time with pencil dots representing the points where the pointing-off machine has been used. The sculptor himself then takes a hand, and with mallet and chisel, with rasp and file, and sometimes sandpaper or shark-skin, gives the forms their final surface and their final expression. The sculptors of the Renaissance probably made nothing more than the merest sketch, perhaps only a drawing, and carved their statues out of the solid block without mechanical aids.

For a bas-relief, or an *alto-relievo*, a background surface of clay or plasteline is prepared, not by any means necessarily flat, upon which the composition is sketched with a stick or a lead-pencil or a tool, and the forms built up on the background with more clay or plasteline, and refined and scraped away to the point of finish where a plaster cast may be made of it, the plaster worked over as for a figure in the round, and then cast in bronze or carved in stone or marble. The treatment given the forms and details must be appropriate to the material.

Coins and medals are merely small bas-reliefs. They are frequently, too frequently, modelled at a size far larger than execution. The medals of Pisanello, done in the fifteenth century, are the finest ever made; and it is quite evident from many indications besides the breadth and simplicity of their design and treatment, that they were modelled at the size of execution. When the original model is made much larger than the finished medal is to be, and then mechanically reduced, the tendency is toward too much detail. When modelled at actual size it is usually done in hard modelling wax. Medals are cast in bronze, silver, and gold, and also struck in a die. Modern coins are always struck; old Greek and Roman coins were cast.

Such, in a brief and general way, are the technical processes by which the sculptor translates a dream into reality. Neither here nor in the description of the architect's methods have we attempted to give any idea of how the artist's mind works through these processes and produces a work of beauty in spite of the mechanical methods, the slow series of steps, he must employ. That would be quite impossible to convey; the mind of every artist works in a different way and modifies methods accordingly.

Many sculptors, and among them some of the very best, began as studio boys or helpers, sweeping up, keeping the clay in the bin and the clay models wet, making themselves generally useful, modelling a little when they had time, until gradually, with this experience and work in night classes in drawing or modelling from the life, they became skilful craftsmen. Others, of course, began in schools of art, supplemented by experience as helpers. When a sculptor is successful and has many and large commissions, it is physically impossible for him to do all of the work himself, and he therefore has assistants who carry out his instructions—good schooling, of course, for them. This has always been so, and there is no doubt that Phidias had a large corps of assistants for his work on the Acropolis of Athens and elsewhere.

The sculptor's studio is usually a pretty rough sort of place, where much heavy work is done, the floor often wet and covered with clay or plaster—as far removed from the popular idea of a studio as possible. It is a place where dreams are dreamed, to be sure; but you would never know it except as you see them made visible in the creations of the artist. Like the architect's office, and the studio of the serious painter, it is pervaded by a professional, not a dilettante, atmosphere; it is a place where a man quietly and without pose does his daily work of creating beauty.

CHAPTER VII

THE TECHNIQUE OF PAINTING

The Training of the Painter — The Materials He Uses — Tempera — Fresco — Oil-painting — Surfaces, Palettes, Brushes, Knives, and Media — How a Painting Is Begun — Glazing — Direct Painting — Impressionism and the Vibration of Light — Mural Painting — Puvis de Chavannes and His Technique — Expression in Mural Painting.

IN all but exceptional and infrequent cases the painter is nowadays the product of the art school. Occasionally a painter will accept a pupil and permit him or her to work in his studio; in days past this was the usual thing. At the school the student draws at first from plaster casts of antique sculpture and, when he has progressed sufficiently, from the living model. These drawings are made on paper with sticks of willow charcoal. When a student is able to draw correctly, and to translate the relative values of the subject—that is, the relation of the darkest dark to the highest light, and of the intermediate lights and darks to both—he is allowed to paint. This training in drawing and painting is rightly begun indoors with simple objects in a strong, cold, steady light. The light out-of-doors is too complicated for the beginner. This is the road all painters follow; they may turn out to be painters of landscape in which not a figure is to be found; but they have been through this indispensable training of the hand and eye—of the eye, to see and analyze the light and shade which is form, and of the hand to render that which the eye perceives. As in Architecture and Sculpture, drawing is at the very founda-

74

tion of Painting. It is the combination of good drawing with good color and good pattern that makes good Painting.

The technique of Painting is very complicated in itself and is further complicated by the fact that nearly every painter has his own methods. The literature on the subject is already voluminous, therefore I shall give here only some general indications of processes and materials. In modern painting there are three or four media used: oil-color, water-color, tempera, and distemper. Practically the same dry colored powders are used for all, but are ground up: for oil-color, with oil—linseed-oil in this country, principally poppy-seed oil in France; for water-color, with water—and glycerine to keep the color soft; mixed with vinegar and egg for tempera and with glue-water for distemper. The powders are made from various minerals, chemicals, or vegetable substances.

Tempera was, before the invention of oil-painting, the medium in which the works of the early Italian school were done, both easel and mural painting; but the technical difficulties of handling it are considerable and troublesome and it is little used at the present day.

We may as well, at this point, dispose briefly of fresco painting as originally practised. Fresco means, in Italian, fresh; and the term was applied to painting on fresh plaster. The great vaults and walls of the Sistine Chapel and many another series of paintings in Italy were done in fresco. The material for the final coat of plaster was very carefully prepared under the eye of the painter, who decided how much surface he could cover in a given time, and applied the plaster to that area. He undoubtedly had his drawing made in advance, and transferred it to the fresh plaster and then painted it in with a form of tempera color; the plaster being damp, the color soaked in and became incorporated with it. This required very rapid and sure execution.

The process of painting in oil-color was invented about the beginning of the fifteenth century; credit for the invention is variously bestowed. It sprang into immediate favor in Venice, and the works of Bellini, Titian, Veronese, and Tintoretto are painted in oil, while the Florentine school, which included Michael Angelo, clung to tempera and fresco. The resources of oil-color are so many, it is handled with so much ease and freedom as compared with the other media, the effects are so immediate or can be predicated with such certainty, it has so much body, richness, and transparency, that the most important work of the present day is done in it.

What follows is to be understood as applying to oil-painting, unless definitely stated not to be.

Almost any kind of surface may be used to paint upon. Wooden panels were once largely used, but they warp and split in the course of time. The most generally satisfactory surface is linen canvas, stretched tightly on a wooden frame called a stretcher or strainer. The canvas is sized with thin glue to keep the oil away from the fibres of the canvas, which linseed-oil rots and burns. It is then usual to prime it with one or two light coats of oil paint and set it away to dry; the priming coat is, as the word indicates, the first or primary coating. Some painters prefer an absorbent ground to paint upon, and coat canvas or panel with a mixture of glue and whiting—which, by the way, was the usual ground the painters in tempera used.

For a surface to mix his colors upon, the painter uses one of several sorts with the generic name of palette. Some use a piece of glass laid flat upon a table; others, a large thin sheet of mahogany or walnut, sometimes oblong, sometimes oval, with a hole in it for the thumb. The colors come in tubes, and are squeezed out on the palette in a certain order which is called "setting the palette." This order varies with the painter. One may put white on the extreme left, and then the lighter colors like the yellows, then the oranges, reds, browns, greens, blues, and finally black at the extreme right. Another may follow the sequence of the colors in the spectrum, beginning at the left with red, then orange, yellow, green, blue, and violet. White would still be at the extreme left, and black, if used, at the right. I say "if used," because more and more as the laws of light and color are better understood, black is being banished from the palette, except in mural painting, where it may be needed for its powerful decorative value.

Some painters use one medium and some another to thin the paint, such as turpentine, colloquially known as "turps," benzine, refined petroleum, thin varnish, or a combination of oils and varnishes. Other men prefer to use the paint as the thick paste in which it comes from the tube, and even extract the oil from it with blotting-paper to make it less fluid.

The color is transferred from the palette to the canvas with brushes of hair or bristle, some flat in shape and some round, and of varying widths and sizes. Some men use a palette-knife to the exclusion of brushes—either the thin flexible knife with which the color is mixed on the palette, or specially shaped and tempered painting-knives.

When a painter begins a picture the procedure is about as follows: he takes a primed canvas, sets it on his easel, and with a piece of charcoal or a brush dipped in thin color draws in the subject. If in charcoal, he "fixes" it, to prevent its rubbing off, with a thin solution of shellac, called fixatif. He then paints in, in a broad and simple way, the principal shadows, then the half-tones—the tones midway between the darkest and the lightest parts—and finally the lights and high lights. This is not always done all at one time. When as much as may be safely done at the first painting is accomplished, the painting is set away to dry to a point where it may be worked on again. A painter usually keeps several canvases going at once for this reason. When a canvas previously begun is taken up again he further refines upon the first blocking in, correcting the drawing, the values, the color, and their interrelations, until it is carried as far as he wishes. This is a very summary statement and does not include a hundred things that a complete treatise on oil-painting would deal with. In the bibliography will be found some titles that will be useful to those who would like to know more than our scope permits us to give.

When the painting is finished it is frequently varnished, more or less heavily, according to the painter's method, or waxed and polished.

We may touch upon one or two more matters just here that will assist in a better comprehension of the paintings you may examine in the museums and galleries. In the early days of painting, and indeed up to very recent times, it was the practice to paint and completely model the subject in some gray or brown, cold or warm, monotone. By "model" we mean: to paint all the light and shade of the forms. When this monotone painting was thoroughly dry it was lightly varnished, and when the varnish was dry, "glazes" of color, that is to say, pure pigment mixed with varnish and oil to make and keep it transparent, were painted or rubbed over the monotone lights and shadows. The glazes being transparent, the modelling of the monotone painting, all its light and shade, showed through them. Other glazes were subsequently carried over the whole or parts of the first glazes, and wonderful and transparent tones were built up in this way. Many of the old Italian, Dutch, and Flemish masterpieces are so built up. To sum up this process, painting a picture was divided into two stages—the first being to paint the light and shade only, and the second, to paint the color only.

Modern painters with few exceptions discard this beautiful but slow and laborious technique as a complete system in favor of "direct" painting, wherein the light and shade and color are all rendered at the same time. This is due to the discoveries made in the vibration of light and the use of broken color, and even the texture of rough paint, to render the aspects of nature. The Impressionist school, headed by Claude Monet, a landscapist, and Edouard Manet, a figure-painter, in the closing years of the nineteenth century, cast aside the old academic formulas and painted nature as they believed it actually to be. Monet especially became interested in problems of light; he and his friends uttered the dictum that "the light is the principal personage" in any picture, landscape, or figure. Analyzing sunlight and shadow and the colors of natural objects, their keen, trained eyes perceived that the effect of what seemed to be a green tree could not be rendered by the use of green paint; that there are other colors in this green tree—blue, yellow, violet, red. So, by placing small areas of pure unmixed color side by side on the canvas, the eye blends them at the right focal distance into the tone which most people with eyes untrained think is the color of the tree and which, if painted entirely in that solid color, would not properly represent that tree. These were revolutionary theories at the time, and feeling ran high between the official, academic faction, and the innovators and their friends. Slowly the truths they contended and suffered for have prevailed, and the debt of the world to

Monet, Pisarro, Sisley, and their group is freely and universally acknowledged.

The differences between the school in France immediately preceding the birth of the so-called Impressionist idea and the exponents of the latter, may be summed up by saying: that the Impressionists went direct to nature for information, and thought for themselves, whereas the Academic school used old recipes for producing effects handed down in the studios and to which they clung; that the Impressionists painted, whether indoors or out, directly from the object or scene they were depicting; where the old school painted always in the cold north light of the studio, with a conventional, assumed, and artificial lighting of the subject instead of the light of out-of-doors; that the Impressionists used pure fresh color put on in such a way as to envelop the subject in light and air; the old school clung to the "brown sauce" of its period—brown sauce being a kind of brown tone used for all shadows, no matter what the color of the object. Some of the Impressionist paintings that looked so boldly revolutionary in 1890 seem conservative enough now; but the Impressionists took the academic bandages from the eyes of the world of art and taught it to see color and to paint the light.

Mural Painting does not aim at the rendition of the truth of nature, and its technique is quite different from that of easel painting. It will be remembered that Mural Painting, being closely related to Architecture, partakes of its nature and is subject to many of its laws; the object is to embellish the surface of an important structural feature of the building; not to pierce it, but preserve the sense that the wall still exists. A drawing of the panel or space, with the architectural elements about it, is made at such a scale that the whole effect may be easily grasped no matter how large the finished picture is to be, and a sketch of the big masses and lines of the composition made upon it, and studied and restudied until Harmony, Balance, and Rhythm between these lines and masses and the lines and masses of the room are established. The sketch is then enlarged and a more careful study of details and of color pattern and masses made. These sketches are made on paper, or cardboard, or canvas, in charcoal, pastel, water-color, or oil-color. Special details of separate figures are then made, usually from life, and frequently at the scale of execution. A great piece of canvas has been prepared on a stretcher; the canvas for large mural paintings is usually woven specially, to avoid joints and seams. Some painters prepare a complete cartoon, as it is called, of the whole picture at full size on paper, and then transfer it to the canvas by one of the several methods of transferring. Others merely mark off their studies, full size or at smaller scale, into squares which bear a proportional relation to similar squares marked off on the canvas, and re-draw their picture on the latter by the aid of these squares and the lines forming them. Others take a small scale drawing, put it in a kind of giant magic lantern, throw the image up to the size they want, and draw it by following the lines of the projected image. The picture entirely drawn, it is ready to paint.

A Mural Painting finished, it is affixed to the wall with a heavy coat of white lead and varnish, spread thickly on the plaster with a trowel.

Where, in an easel picture, the edges of objects would be softened, "lost" as the painter says, the forms in a mural painting are outlined with a strong outline. In brief, a mural painting is more like a large colored drawing than like an easel picture.

There is as wide a divergence in Mural Painting as there

is in easel painting, in theory, method, and treatment, and we may do no better than to describe some of the methods of the greatest of all modern mural painters, Puvis de Chavannes. He preserves the sense of the wall and yet attains a sense of depth and perspective, and avoids the flat and papery effect of a poster, partly by his treatment of light and shade, partly by his handling of values, partly by his color. His color is cool and gray and its range has been aptly described as his "lilac chord." Lilacs, blues, and grey blues, grey greens, cool yellows, cool, but often rich reds, are his palette. His values are "close"; that is to say, a figure robed in blue in the foreground is little different in value from one farther back in the picture also robed in blue. There are no violent contrasts. In one of his panels in the Hôtel de Ville or City Hall of Paris, some trees in the background are just about as dark as the group of men in the foreground, but the two take their proper places by reason of the way they are drawn; by this device he secured the effect of depth and perspective in his drawing and yet brought the distant plane in which the trees lie up to the first plane (the plane of the wall) with his color values. His pictures are bathed in a soft, diffused light—"the light that never was on land or sea"—and his figures have their being in an enchanted land. And while each object and figure is modelled in light and shade in itself, it is to be observed that they cast no shadows on other figures or objects. A little darkening of the ground at the feet of a figure, a touch of dark where the butt of a staff touches the ground, suffices to locate it on the ground plane. His drawing is simplified in a remarkable and very personal manner; his preliminary studies for the separate figures of his compositions are accurate transcripts from nature, but he translates them, by subjecting them to a process of simplification, into something quite different, sculptural in its massive strength. And thus, by the strength of his drawing and the masculine quality of his forms, the delicacy of his color is redeemed from any sense of weakness; were his drawing not as virile and rugged as it is his color might seem too ethereal.

One of the masters of Mural Painting of the Renaissance, Pintoricchio, attains a sense of decorative flatness and conventionalization by modelling certain portions in relief and gilding them. This followed the old tradition of illuminated books, and Pintoricchio may have adopted the treatment through the influence of the paintings of Gentile da Fabriano and Benozzo Gozzoli, both of whom made a similar use of gilded relief, and both of whom were in their turn influenced by the work of Fra Angelico.

CHAPTER VIII

THE TECHNIQUE OF OTHER VEHICLES OF EXPRESSION

Distemper—Water-color — Miniatures — Monotypes—Pastels—Etchings — Steel Engravings — Copperplate Engravings — Mezzotint Engravings — Wood Engravings — Japanese Prints — Linoleum Block Prints — Lithography.

A BRIEF description of some of the other vehicles of expression will make this summary of technical processes sufficiently complete for our purpose.

Distemper is the material used nowadays in what is commonly and erroneously called fresco painting—the tinting of plaster walls and ceilings. Dry powdered color is mixed for use with glue water as a binder. It is the medium in which the scene painter works. It is very ready and rapid, and vast surfaces are quickly covered; a good scene painter will knock off a back-drop thirty or forty feet square in three or four days.

For water-color painting the colors come either in little tubes or china pans. Water is used to dissolve them to such a consistency that they may be used in a brush. The pigments are of different weights and degrees of fineness in grinding, some being made of mineral, others of vegetable, substances, and still others of chemical derivatives, and the particles of powder deposit themselves on the paper in ways peculiar to each. While the colored powder is fresh and wet it looks much darker and more brilliant than when dry, and the painter must, therefore, allow at all times for this change and know the characteristics of his pigments so well that he may make them do his will. There are two general methods of painting in water-color, transparent and opaque; in the one, the color is used as a transparent wash on white paper which supplies the white necessary for dilution; in the other, an opaque white pigment made of zinc—Chinese White—renders the mixture opaque, the white pigment supplying that required, as in oil-painting. The brushes used are usually round, of sable or of camel's hair; flat bristle or hair brushes are preferred by some painters, and give a distinctive character to the work done with them.

Miniatures are very small paintings in oil or water-color upon wood, parchment, ivory, or other surfaces. Modern miniatures and indeed the best of the older ones are painted upon ivory in water-color. A true miniature is never more than three or four inches square at the utmost; when larger it ceases to have that precious and jewel-like quality which is one of its greatest charms. While it requires exquisite skill of hand and eye to paint at so small a scale, a miniature must not be confused in kind with those mere miracles of patience exemplified by the cherry-stone carved with one hundred and forty distinguishable heads. Though small in scale and compass they are susceptible of great breadth of treatment as well as great delicacy.

A monotype is, as the name implies, a single impression, on a piece of paper, of a painting done in oil-color on a sheet of glass or metal. When well done it is very interesting and distinctive in character. The painting is made in very thin pigment to avoid spreading when printed, and the brush strokes and handling are made to play an important part in the final effect. A piece of paper is dampened and laid over the painting and a roller passed over the back of the paper. The pressure transfers the paint to the paper and the dampness prevents the oil in the paint from spreading and staining the margins. It is a fascinating process and a pleasant relaxation from more serious work, because there are so many accidents, some happy, some the reverse. Sometimes the most carefully made monotype is a complete failure and the one dashed off with no especial care is a great success. Some painters touch up their impressions afterward, but this is not true monotype technique.

Pastels are colored powders made up into sticks with a binder of glue or gum-water, in varying degrees of softness and hardness. The painter draws with them upon paper, cardboard, or canvas, and upon surfaces specially prepared with fine sand or felt. The most exquisite things have been done in them. They are dainty and delicate and demand a dainty and delicate technique. Chardin's paintings in pastel are famous and have all the solidity and strength of oils. Whistler, on the other hand, made pastels of the most fragile and tenuous nature. Pastel paintings are perishable, not because they fade, for they are remarkably durable in that sense, but because the powder may be so easily shaken or jarred off the surface to which it is applied. They must be carefully kept under glass, and gently handled. When fixatif is applied, in the effort to keep the powder fast, the freshness which is one of the beauties of the medium disappears, and the drawing takes on the dull and flat quality of a painting in distemper.

An etching is an impression of a drawing either scratched in a plate of copper or zinc with a strong steel needle, or bitten in with acid; thick ink is then rubbed into the incised lines; the plate is wiped off, put in a special press, and printed on dampened paper under great pressure. When the lines are bitten in with acid, the impression is called an etching. When they are scratched into the metal with a tool, and no acid used, the print is called a dry-point.

To make a dry-point, the drawing, or the principal lines of it, is made either directly upon the copper, or upon paper and transferred. Some artists darken the plate so that they may readily see the scratched-in lines. The cutting tool, known under the generic name of needle, raises a burr along every line which takes the ink and gives a certain blur and richness to the line when printed. The skilful etcher makes this burr play an important part in his technique.

To make an etching, the copper is coated with a kind of varnish, very thin, but impermeable by the acid, and blackened by passing a smoky wax taper across the face. The drawing is then made with the etching-needle which scratches through the coating of varnish and leaves the surface of the copperplate exposed. When the drawing is complete, the plate is coated on the back and edges with the grounding varnish and is immersed in a shallow tray of dilute nitric acid which eats into the copper. When the lines which are to be the lightest and finest in the print are bitten deep enough, the plate is removed from the acid bath, washed thoroughly in clean water, and these lightest lines painted over with a brush dipped in stopping-out varnish. Then the plate is put back in the bath to be bitten again for the lines that are to be the next darkest; washed; that series of lines stopped out; and this process continued until the darkest lines have been, by a series of immersions in the acid, bitten quite deep. If a line is wrong, or if an imperfection in the coating has permitted the acid to attack the plate, the copper is scraped away with the offending line or spot in it, the plate turned over on a soft pad, the back of it struck so as to restore the level of the surface on the right side, and the place repolished, made perfect again, and that portion of the plate re-etched. When all the lines are etched to a point where the etcher's experience tells him they are about right, he cleans off the coating, polishes the plate with whiting, and it is ready to ink and print.

By another process the plate is immersed so that a shallow film of very weak acid covers it. Those lines and portions which are to be darkest in the print are drawn first and then the lighter ones in their proper succession. The acid begins to act at once so that the first lines drawn are quite deeply bitten by the time the last and lightest are begun. This, as may be imagined, requires great powers of visualization and immense skill.

The process of printing is the same for dry-points and etchings. The ink, a thick ink of brownish black tone as a rule, is spread on a slab and with a pad like a ball is transferred to the plate and worked thoroughly into the etched or scratched lines. Some etchers use the ball of the thumb for this, as a more sensitive implement. Then the plate is wiped—one of the most delicate steps in the process, for a great deal of the effect of the impression depends upon it. Some men like a cleanly wiped plate and depend solely upon the lines for effect. Others leave a film of ink over most of the plate, frequently heavier at the corners. Resort is had also to *retroussage*: the plate being warmed and the thus softened ink lifted out of the grooves of the lines a little with a piece of soft gauze, the effect is to soften the lines and blur them a trifle. In dry-points the plate is so inked that the burr is made a great deal of.

The plate inked, it is then put on the bed of the press, the dampened paper laid over it and covered with two or three heavy felt or woollen blankets. The etcher seizes one of the long arms which radiate from the hub of the roller and, pulling it over, the bed of the press is caused to pass under the rollers—which may be adjusted to any degree of pressure—the blankets turned back, the paper removed. The pressure is enormous, and has forced the damp paper into the etched grooves and the ink in them has been transferred to the paper. The etcher examines the impression with critical care, and then begins a series of re-bitings, of lightening or darkening portions or single lines, with trial proofs taken until he feels he can do no more to improve it. In exhibitions of etchings the student may often see impressions catalogued as "first state," "second state," and so on. These are some of the trial proofs of which we speak, and are of absorbing interest to those who love etchings.

Steel engravings and copperplate engravings are made on steel or copper plates, with a tool called a burin, which cuts a clean groove in the metal. The steel plates are then hardened; and prints are made somewhat as etchings are printed, except that the plate is wiped clean.

In mezzotint engraving a toothed rocker of steel is passed over a copper plate in all directions in such a manner as to roughen it all over equally and create a burr. The grain so made is cut and burnished away. The engraver works from dark to light by removing the grain to a greater or lesser degree, the untouched grain giving approximately black; pure white is secured by scraping the grain entirely away. Line is dispensed with, and only masses, with gradations of light and shade, are aimed at.

The wood engraver cuts away those portions of the surface which he does not want to receive the ink, leaving the lines which are to be printed in relief. Boxwood, a very hard substance, is the usual surface. The subject is drawn or photographed on the wood first and then patiently engraved. The cut is inked with a roller as type is inked. When a great many impressions are required, metal electrotypes are made of the block, and these are used to print from instead of the precious wood block. The Japanese print is a woodcut, separate blocks made for the lines of the drawing, and for each color. The Japanese use the face grain of a board very often in these color blocks for the sake of the texture the grain gives. In the boxwood blocks referred to above, the end grain of the wood is used.

Akin to woodcuts in principle are linoleum block prints. The linoleum, plain linoleum like that on kitchen floors, is fastened to a board, the drawing made upon it or transferred to it, and the linoleum cut away with small gouges such as wood-carvers use. It is inked with a roller, with printer's ink or oil paint, and printed by passing a printer's hand roller over the back of the dampened paper. Separate blocks are used for the drawing and for each color as in Japanese prints.

A lithograph is a print, in a greasy lithographic ink, from a drawing made with ink or crayon, upon a fine-grained limestone having a peculiar affinity for grease. This property of the stone was discovered by accident in 1719 by a man named Senefelder who thereupon invented and developed the processes still in use. These processes are many and complicated—far too complex to attempt to describe here with any degree of clarity. It must suffice to say that a drawing is made either upon the stone, or upon a specially prepared paper and transferred to the stone, with greasy lithographic ink or crayon, and after etching the stone with acid, and treating it with gum-water, the stone may be inked with a roller. Those parts of the stone which have received the grease of the drawing will take the ink and the rest of the wet surface refuse it. The impression is made in a special press. It is a cheap and rapid method of reproducing very complicated designs in black and white or colors, from labels on cans to theatrical posters of great size, and has perhaps fallen into disrepute with artists on that account.

But it is an art which combines great power with the extreme of delicacy, rich velvety blacks and exquisite silvery greys; and in every generation men have been found who produced beautiful things in it—Isabey, Bonington, Roberts, Gavarni, Ropps, Whistler.

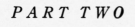

PART TWO

CHAPTER IX

BEFORE THE CURTAIN

Art as a Part of the Fabric of Human Life — Inventions and Their Influence upon the History of Art — Climate and Great World Forces — Human Nature in All Ages Alike — A Summary of Artistic History — A Pageant of the Egyptian and Mesopotamian Worlds.

IN the preceding pages I have given some notion of the nature of art, of the artist's point of view, and of the way he does his work. Those which follow are intended as the briefest possible introduction to the history of art, merely to indicate and suggest its relations to the major movements of the history of mankind, and serve, I hope, to stimulate the reader to a much more extended study.

The history of art is too often written of as an isolated phenomenon unrelated to the facts of life; there could be no error more grave. Art is integral with the fabric of life. It is not a separate stream running parallel with the current of human events; it is one of the threads of that current, and the sweep of life and the progress of art are identical in movement.

When reading of the past it is difficult to bear in mind that steam and electricity are of such recent use; that printing was unknown in Europe until 1438 shortly after the introduction of paper manufacture from China; that transportation and communication was by means of galleys rowed with oars, or by rude sailing vessels so small one wonders at the temerity that attempted the voyages they weathered; or by camel or horse or ox wain; that there were no post-offices until the reign of Louis XI in France. And that the telegraph and telephone, both wired and wireless; the phonograph, the typewriter, the monotype and linotype machines, and all such means of rapidly duplicating and recording writing and speech; the development of photography; the invention of electric light and power; the aeroplane—all are products of the past fifty years; in short, none of the miracles we have come to regard as commonplaces of existence had come to pass. Ideas and news were circulated slowly and inaccurately, from mouth to mouth. A building, a book, a picture, or a play, finished yesterday, is being discussed to-morrow in every centre that pretends to any tincture of cultivation in the world. Not so in earlier times; and we are obliged to remind ourselves constantly of these vast differences in the circumstances of our own daily life. They explain much that would otherwise be obscure to us in the history of art or of mankind, such as the slow growth and national agreement of style in some countries, contrasted with the development of distinctly marked and differing types in others; the ranges of hills, the wide marshy tracts, or the dense forests, which acted as barriers to the spread of intellectual influences in a more primitive world, and which fostered these agreements or divergences, are now negligible factors in one in which science is year by year sweeping physical barriers aside and making human society homogeneous and cosmopolitan.

The climate of a country or of a district, the daily life and social customs of a people, the ease or difficulty of intercourse with other peoples or with communities of like race far or near, the plants, the birds, the beasts, the quality and kind of building material, the scarcity of wood, the absence of stone, the presence of clay, the inherited traditions of the inhabitants, these and many other factors act, react, and interact upon the arts of any given place or period. To these we must add the influence a work of art has in it-

Three types of GREEK VASES. The central one is an Amphora, or two-handled jar for holding provisions, with red figures on a black ground, dating from 470–450 B. C. That on the left is an Oinochoë, or wine jug, of the sixth century. On the right is a Lekythos, or oil jug, of the years 500–480 B. C.

The CRESTING of the THOLOS at EPIDAUROS, a circular secular building of the fourth century, B. C., by POLYCLEITOS THE YOUNGER; illustrating the use of geometrical patterns as ornament in conjunction with that derived from vegetable and animal forms.

self upon those which follow it. Then we must reckon with political and humanistic movements; the influence of religions; the migrations and dispersions of races; invasions, wars; the character, tastes, and ambitions of rulers; trade by land and sea. The simplest bit of architecture, painting, sculpture, pottery, or textile that comes to mind is the child of all these forces.

But beneath the veil of outward circumstance human nature in all its fundamental qualities and defects is much the same as it was centuries and centuries ago. We respond to similar emotions and impulses—we hunger, we thirst, we shiver, we sweat, we feel remorse or joy, we are proud or humble, vain or modest, good, bad, or indifferent, just like some one else in the childhood of the world. There is no reason for us to feel that the men and the arts of distant times are really a long way off. The seeing eye views the men and women and children of all time not as pale and bloodless spectres, but as warm and sentient human creatures with all their differentiated qualities and defects; sees them moving to and fro about their affairs in the streets formed by and framed in the architecture with which we have learned to be familiar; and then we realize that the jamb of this old doorway, that old wall, are worn and polished by the actual, personal, physical contact of scores of generations of human beings; only thus may we humanize the otherwise lifeless stone. We must go to the play with these fellow beings, sit with them in house or hall, listen to their bards in their company, join with them in fight or frolic.

The history of Western architecture may be summed up in a paragraph; and the arts of painting and sculpture, and the divers arts related to them and to architecture, fall within similar categories: first emerges the Grecian with the Egyptian and Assyrian from which it principally derives in the background, all three based upon a post and lintel system of construction; next the Roman, which adds the arch, its blood brother the vault, and its cousin the dome, probably borrowed by the Romans from Etruscan and Persian sources; then the Romanesque, little more than an ignorant or naïf use of Roman forms; the Byzantine, contemporary toward the East with the Romanesque in the West and blending Grecian, Asian, and Roman elements; the Arabic, Saracenic, and Moorish, evolved by the Mohammedans from Persian origins; then the Mediæval or Gothic, that glorious flowering of the Romanesque, Byzantine, and Saracenic stocks into a highly organized structural system of isolated supports and balanced thrusts, with light screen-walls between the piers as enclosures; then a reversion to Roman forms in the Renaissance, of which the sequent progress is checked by the French Revolution; since then, an eclecticism in which no convictions are apparent, but in essence a continuation of the Renaissance impulse. We may therefore recognize broadly three major periods in modern Western art—the Classic, comprising Grecian and Roman works and their immediate derivatives; Mediæval or Gothic; and the Renaissance, now gathering new force again after the lapse of more than a century.

These are only convenient chapter headings, as it were, for the clearer arrangement of our subject-matter. We may only roughly refer a style to a certain span of years. There are penumbræ of transition at each end of it and around it, reactions upon it of the style that is growing out of it, throw-backs to the style from which it issued, sporadic interjections of foreign motifs explicable only by the play and counterplay of international relations—many like circumstances that burst through the limits of categories. I remember a time when I had a vague impression that the

Kings of France in person had had a good deal to do with the invention of the styles called by their names and that the day Louis XIV died, the Style Louis XV began. I use the term invention in that connection because it marks a frequent misconception—no style was ever invented; a style develops by processes obscure, and cannot be consciously directed.

Art may be conceived as one great stream flowing down to us from ancient times through many lands coloring its waters as it passes, here running crystal clear, there spreading wide and reflecting the sky, now moving sullenly in a narrow channel—but, though swelled by many tributaries, always sweeping on, always the same stream. And the traveller must have some means of knowing through what territory he is passing; that just about here we are leaving Romanesque country and entering upon Gothic; that the sunny range we see far off down-stream is the land of the Renaissance and that it will recall to us in many ways the bright hills of Hellas we passed not long ago. The arts may seem, superficially viewed, to be swayed by surface currents—and in the lesser movements may be—but their general trend responds to forces or a sum of forces hidden perhaps very deeply, as a sunken rock or fault in the river-bed may cause an eddy on the surface. The trend of a period of art must be viewed as a whole and compared as a whole with the tendencies of its epoch as a whole.

Beyond the first Olympiad, beginning 776 B. C., tracing as it does the first dim line discernible between the historic and the prehistoric, we need not attempt to penetrate deeply in the brief review of the history of art we propose. Let it be as though, arriving a little late at a pageant, we miss a part of the prologue and find the depths of the stage shut off by thickness upon thickness of gauze dropped plane by plane until the eye can pierce no farther. The light is dim. It is the dawn of the history of the modern world and in its faint light we see shadowy forms astir and hear ghostly voices; as the centuries pass in review the light grows stronger, the personages more distinct, the voices clearer, the action richer in incident. Of the scenes played after our entrance the first are laid in Egypt, in Babylonia, and Assyria; they serve as an introduction to the play of action in the modern world marked by the entrance of the Greeks upon the stage of history.

The curtain rises upon the long lines of the Egyptian Kings, dynasty beyond dim dynasty vanishing into the mists of the past; pyramids violet against the orange of the desert sky; great temples where incense rises to gods long since forgotten; we behold Egypt in her glory—then the scene changes and she appears in chains, her proud neck bowed down beneath a foreign yoke. We see Psammetichus with the aid of Greek mercenaries cast off that yoke, drive out the hated foreigner, and Egypt become the instructress of Greece. Psammetichus passes; his son Necho the Second comes upon the stage and before his reign is over the realm becomes tributary to Babylon, later lies prostrate beneath the heel of Persia, regains once more her independence and loses it at last to Alexander; she accepts the Greeks, her erstwhile pupils, as her masters and finally is absorbed with them into the all-conquering Roman Empire.

Again the scene changes, from the valley of the Nile to an immense and fertile plain between the Tigris and the Euphrates, threaded with canals for irrigation and for commerce, channels built in the sweat and cemented in the blood of countless slaves. Across the shimmering fields dim shapes of cities rise, lifted above the gleaming levels on vast artificial mounds; the palaces of Kings, the gardens of Queens terraced to the skies arise to the sound of whips in the hands of the dark overseers lashing the backs of men driven beyond their strength. And on this mighty stage the drama that extended over seven centuries: the King returning from the hunt, the whirling chariots of his suite raising columns of dust that mount to heaven; the King returning from his wars with captive monarchs at his chariot wheels, a long and mournful tail of myriads of their subjects stretching to the horizon. The Assyrians, led by Tiglath-Pileser the Third, conquer Babylonia; Babylon is obliterated and her people enslaved. Nineveh is adorned in the reigns of Sennacherib and Asshur-bani-pal, and Assyria under these sovereigns combines the innumerable petty tribes and states of Western Asia and spreads among them the civilization borrowed from Babylonia. Led by Nabopolassar, the Babylonians rise against Assyria, and Nineveh falls and after the terrors of the sack returns into the desert; the lion and the jackal prowl about her courts; and two hundred years later Xenophon passes the place with his Ten Thousand and cannot learn even her name.

The new Babylonian Empire endures for threescore years and ten, and in that time Babylon becomes the wonder of the ancient world. Then, out of the Northeast, the hordes of the Medes and Persians of Cyrus descend like a cloud upon the land and Babylon in her turn is given to the flames, her hanging gardens wither and perish, her water-courses dry up, her lofty structures of sun-dried brick, roofless, become again one with the dust of the plain; and with her passing the sceptre of domination wielded so long by the Semitic race is grasped by the hands of Aryan peoples, in those hands to remain.

CHAPTER X

THE GREEKS APPEAR

The Entrance of the Greeks upon the Stage of History — The Hellenic World — Characteristics of the Greeks — The Qualities of Their Art — Abstraction — Freedom — Refinements of Athenian Architecture — Archaic Sculpture — Its Polychrome Treatment — The Use of Color in Architecture and Sculpture — Praxiteles and Nicias.

THE light grows stronger. A land appears, seamed with valleys between high ranges of hills, its coasts now rugged, now shelving in sandy beaches washed by the "wine-dark sea," deeply indented by bays and gulfs, almost barren of trees save the olive and the spired cypress, the stubborn soil refusing to yield much more than the fruit of the vine, sparse crops of grain, and a scanty pasturage for goats, sheep, or cattle. A land of purple and gold and blue—the purple of the hills clothed in bay, the gold of the soil, the ineffable, triumphant blue of the sky; of a singular and austere loveliness, designed on broad and simple lines that give the illusion of great scale to a landscape containing no elements of unusual size. Such is the land of Greece, the homeland of the Hellenes.

Politically a mere congeries of cities, debarred by racial origins and by the conformation of the country from true national life, banding together for mutual help against common foes when threatened from without, fighting savagely among themselves at other times, their spiritual tie their religion, their typical trait a fierce sense of independence, and deep-rooted in their souls the passion for self-government. Protected on the north from the barbarian hordes by lofty mountains easy of defense; on the west and south by the open sea; linked to the Asian shores by the archipelago which, island by lovely island, had been the stepping-stones of their progress beyond the veil of antiquity. In such a land and under such conditions were the Hellenes nurtured.

Their origins are lost to us. We know that broadly speaking they issued from two sources to be classed as Dorian and Ionian, of which the Spartans and Athenians are typical—the Dorian Spartans, the Prussians of Greece, warlike, predatory, caring little for the graces of life; the Ionian Athenians, to whom art, beauty, literature, and the drama were as important elements of life as war and politics. All Greeks from the Black Sea to Marseilles were proud to call themselves Hellenes—but the Athenian was first of all a citizen of Athens, an Argive a citizen of Argolis, and there was no nation in our modern sense. The life of the many tribes centred in the cities, walled for defense against their jealous and quarrelsome neighbors, and surrounded with a certain area of tillable soil to which the laborers repaired during the day, returning to the shelter of the city walls at night like the contadini of Italy or the peasants of France. Although the finest flower of the intellectual life of the Hellenes blossomed in Athens, she was even at her prime merely the focal point of a wide-spread culture that included the Corinthian, the Ionian of the cities of Asia Minor, the Bœotian, with the garrulous Athenian always eager to tell and hear of some new thing, and the laconic Spartan chary of speech.

Of all the gifts of the gods the most desirable is imagination; to souls endowed with it there are no horizons—they wing into the infinite. The Greeks were so endowed. They heard the voice of Zeus in the storm, the voice of the Naiad in the purling of the brook, and saw Aphrodite born of the foam of the sea. A great and sympathetic critic, Walter Pater, says: "The Greeks' thoughts about themselves and their relation to the world generally were . . . ever ready to be transformed into objects for the senses. In this lies the main distinction between Greek art and the mystical art of the Christian Middle Age which is always struggling to express thoughts beyond itself." The Greeks conceived of their gods as possessing human attributes, human beauty, raised to a higher power; and before they learned to express themselves in terms of beauty their sentiment toward the shapeless wooden images which embodied their early vision of the gods is comparable to the feeling of a child toward the rag doll she endows with every grace and every virtue.

They were men of essentially simple minds, clear thinkers, lucid speakers, but subtle in argument and dialectic; touched with the divine fire of imagination; with a passionate devotion to "form," to beauty, in all things from art to athletics; profound in their knowledge of human nature and the contents of men's souls and the tragedies and comedies of life; and yet, alas, often tainted with dishonesty; faithless; treacherous; envious; fickle; jealous. This is a sort of catalogue of their qualities and as in all catalogues the soul of the thing described escapes; genius is perhaps the one inclusive term that might be used, for genius does not necessarily imply virtue in its possessor.

The Greek race was not composed of personages of surpassing beauty, each more intelligent, more sensitive to harmony than the other; the name Bœotian was a synonym in the mouth of the Athenian for grossness, vulgarity, and stupidity; and the philosopher Socrates was one of the ugliest of men.

They are the first of the modern peoples, although their story is to be found in the Ancient Histories. It was in Greece that the modern mind was born. Greek influences are at work to-day in life, in art, in language; the terminology of logic, natural science, and philosophy is Greek; Grecian art contains within itself, in matured and developed form, the germs, hints, ideas, traditions, derived from Eastern sources—from Egypt, Assyria, Babylonia, and from that dim Minoan civilization, of which we are just beginning to learn, that centred in Crete.

Quality is in all their works—quality and distinction. Their works of architecture have the spirit of their sculpture, quick with life, the soul of beauty expressed in stone. Only the architect, who knows the technical processes through which a work of architecture must be carried— the long road from the first dim adumbration of the idea to the finished structure, the travail of soul, the danger of loss of the spirit of the conception in the mechanical processes involved—only an architect can measure the achievements and equipment of the Greek architect; the extraordinary combination of mathematician and artist, the cool faculties controlling the warm; the delicate adjustment of the parts of the structure to the whole, the patient modulation of form after form, the profound knowledge of optical illusions and their use or cure. In measuring what the Greeks achieved in architecture we may keep in view without disparagement that they were, especially in their temples, engaged in the elaboration of types which, in their general aspects, were fairly fixed and consecrated through long usage. We may trace this in the evolution of the Doric temple through the centuries; Ictinus, the architect of the Parthenon, brought it to its highest pitch of perfection, following the works of a long line of predecessors occupied in the solution of the like problem generation after generation, each adding a little to the sum of architectural knowledge; a better proportion, a refinement here, another there; this or that difficulty better overcome in the next essay.

In all forms of art the Greek genius is marked by measure and restraint, limiting itself to a few motifs, consecrating itself to the development of these to a high and ever higher perfection—in music, the drama, painting, sculpture, architecture. "Measure in all things" was inscribed upon the Temple of the Oracle at Delphi.

In architecture and sculpture the character of the scanty vegetation of the land, the few floral forms at the command of the artist, exerted their powerful but unconscious influence; he was thrown back upon the human figure, the vine, the olive, the laurel, the honeysuckle, the leaves of the acanthus growing wild at the bases of the hills. The heads of bulls, of rams, and occasionally of goats, figure now and then in his designs. These did not quite suffice for his decorative needs and he found delight in abstract arrangements of line in geometrical patterns having no relation to the animal or vegetable kingdoms. The quality of abstraction, however, distinguishes all Greek work. The exquisite oval of a Grecian face, the line from brow to nose tip, the beautiful mouth and chin are largely artistic conventions; the general type existed perhaps, but the artist abstracted the most perfect elements in the type, and having created a new beauty by the rejection of the accidental and the trivial used it as a standard of taste, leaving his genius free to modify it and perfect it. Much of this quality, even after sculpture came to be independently used, is due to the intimate relation it had had to architecture. When the artist of Greece used the human figure, the vine, the laurel, or the olive, he looked upon them as so many forms or shapes, as decorative units, to dissect and recompose as suited the need of the moment, not as limb or leaf, fruit or flower.

Great art so modifies individuality that it takes on the quality of universality; it does not consist in the delineation of merely individual traits in man, beast, or vegetable.

Another salient trait of this art is freedom. Freedom ranging within self-imposed limits, acting under self-imposed laws. The lifeless copies of Grecian architecture, the cold and repellent imitations of Grecian sculptures inflicted upon the world by several Greek revivals have given a false impression not merely of the surface characteristics of Grecian art, but of the very spirit of it. Far from being "icily regular, splendidly null" a Greek temple is full of irregularities deliberately arranged in a regular frame. In the Parthenon, for example, the columns are not spaced at equal distances; as they approach the angles of the temple they are set closer together; the corner columns, which are seen against the sky and which the light therefore seems to consume somewhat by halation, are made thicker to correct this optical illusion; the outline of the columns is not straight but has an exquisite outward curve or entasis; and they diminish in diameter toward the top; the axis lines of all the columns not merely incline backward, but lean toward the centre also to an extent that would cause them to meet at a height of about a mile; the walls incline backward; the stylobate or series of steps on which the columns rest is curved, springing upward toward the centre; the line of the architrave, or lintel stones which rest upon the columns, follows another, similar curve. The only straight lines are those of the pediments or gable ends of the roof, and in the Theseum, built a few years later, these, too, are slightly curved. It is to be particularly remarked that these refinements are of the most subtle sort. They are so far from being obvious that their existence was discovered only during the last generation. But their presence or absence makes just the difference between springing life and the inertia of mere masses of stone. An impression generally prevails among those unfamiliar with Grecian buildings that they were perfectly symmetrical, part balancing part and reproducing each other with fidelity. On the contrary the Greek, artist that he was, adapted the design to the conditions of the site or of the problem; the Erechtheum and the Propylæa, both on the Athenian Acropolis, both of the great period, both the work of Mnesicles, are merely two examples of many that illustrate the freedom of Greek design from any preoccupation with symmetry.

The sculpture is instinct with the same subtle, essential, organic freedom. We have already referred to repose as being an element of great sculpture, and spirited repose is the mark of the Greek. Cold symmetry is absent; examine a Greek head and you will find the subtle differences between eye and eye, brow and brow, cheek and cheek, that occur in nature; and attitudes and expressions are as free from self-consciousness and affectation as they are free from the lackadaisical or the rigid. Of course early Greek sculpture was stiff enough in all conscience. On the Acropolis in Athens is a little Museum containing some of the most precious relics of sculpture we have of the time prior to the destruction of the temples by the Persians; they show what Athenian sculpture was before Phidias; so many of the connecting links between the two periods have been destroyed that upon a cursory view it almost seems as though Attic art leaped from the naïf simplicity of childhood to full maturity at a bound. These statues resemble in spirit the sculptures of the portals of Chartres Cathedral carved in the thirteenth century of the Christian era; they have a similar simple treatment of the draperies and the fixed smiles of primitive sculpture everywhere. The archaic Greek statue was decorated with color, partly no doubt to express what the skill of the carver was at that time inadequate to render or suggest; and artistic criticism is beginning to realize that Mediæval sculpture also was highly polychromatic.

It is easy to see how Greek painting may have developed from the decoration of sculpture and of vases into an independent branch of art; but all vestiges of the paintings of the great periods have disappeared and nothing but legends about them survive. These tales indicate that the Greek painter attained a high degree of skill in the naturalistic representation of nature; Zeuxis deceived the birds who pecked at his grapes, and Parrhasius deceived Zeuxis with a painted curtain. Only faint traces upon fragments remain to suggest what Greek polychromy was. We are assured from many sources that color was used with great freedom in architecture and sculpture. The little figurines of painted terra-cotta found in the tombs at Tanagra in Bœotia and other places, little groups and single figures of a charming grace, indicate in a faint, far-off way, as such things must, how lovely Greek polychrome sculpture of the highest class must have been. Whatever it was, we may be sure that artists with the sense of form as highly developed as the Greeks would not have been found wanting in the matter of color; and in envisaging what is to many persons a new idea it is to be remembered that their temples were placed on rocky eminences running the gamut from ivory to umber, with a setting of purple hills, blue sky, and bluer sea. In a preceding chapter we touched upon the general traits of the sculpture of Praxiteles, in which the most exquisite and subtle modulations of form are to be found, and the world for many years not merely accepted it as perhaps the highest possible excellence to which the treatment of form can rise, but would have been inexpressibly shocked had it been suggested that such perfect form was originally colored—and yet Nicias, a great painter, was also famous as the man who helped Praxiteles color his statues! The fact that the great Praxiteles, sensitive to the ultimate degree in his apprehension and rendition of form, feeling that form was not enough, added color to what seems perfect without it, is for me conclusively in favor of the use of color in sculpture. I am quite willing to believe that the beauty of the color was equal to the beauty of form and that the sum of these two beauties made a third, more piercing, more moving, more marvellous than anything the world has seen since that day.

CHAPTER XI

PERIODS AND PERSONAGES IN GRECIAN ART

Three Periods in Grecian Art — The Pre-Periclean Age — The Temples of Magna Græcia and Sicily — The Use of Stone, Stucco, and Marble — The Traffic in Vases — Defeat of the Persians — The Confederacy of Delos — Pericles and the Golden Age — Phidias — Ictinus — Mnesicles and other Artists — Plato and Socrates — The Post-Periclean Era — Praxiteles — Lysippus — Apelles — The Greek Theatre.

WE may conveniently divide Grecian art into three periods—the pre-Periclean or pre-Phidian—the Golden or Periclean Age with its second blossoming after the death of Pericles—and the Alexandrian Age down to the time when Greece became a Roman Province. Of the first little remains in architecture except some of the ruined temples of Sicily and Southern Italy and even these are but fragmentary. Of them the so-called Basilica and the Temple of Demeter at Pæstum below Pompeii, and the Temple of Concord at Agrigentum in Sicily, are typical. They are the fruit of the age of colonization, that seed-time of Greece, when her cities, of an adventurous and restless spirit, reaching out for trade, were sending out colonies to Sicily, to Southern Italy— known as Magna Græcia or Greater Greece—to the islands to the eastward and northeastward up to the Hellespont and Propontis, and in this relief of the pressure of growing populations coming into contact with her neighbors, learning from them and they from her. It will be observed that these early temples are rude and clumsy in their proportions —but it was from structures such as these that the Parthenon was to be evolved. These temples and many others in provinces remote from marble quarries were built of limestone or of volcanic tufa, neither being susceptible of that high degree of surface finish in which the Greeks delighted, and they therefore covered these rougher stones with a fine hard stucco. I am quite convinced that the Greek architect did not regard marble with the almost superstitious reverence in which it is held by the practitioners of the present day, and did not hesitate to stain and paint it; that he preferred it when obtainable, partly because of its translucent structure but principally because it is easily worked, so that a pure and true arris could be obtained which would cast a pure true shadow on a pure true surface. It is well known, especially to sculptors, that by passing the hand over a surface inequalities and modulations may be perceived that are quite invisible to the eye; when this test is applied to architectural work of the finest period such as the temples on the Athenian Acropolis, it is quite impossible to detect any imperfections of the surface; it is as true as human skill can make it.

In her intercourse with her neighbors during the sixth and fifth centuries before Christ, Athens exported incredible quantities of vases to the countries lying west, particularly to Etruria just north and northwest of Rome. Vases were signed as painters sign their canvases to-day; so we know that a certain Euphronius was one of the most famous of these potters and painters. It is true of all periods that the smaller and more portable objects of use or beauty are those by which the arts of one people become first known to others, through trade and barter, through the presents one ruler may make to another, through the curious or beautiful things travellers bring back to their homes.

The Golden Age was inaugurated by the defeat of the Persians by the Athenians at Salamis within sight of Athens, at Platæa, and at Mycale, in 481–480; Athens became the most splendid city of the Hellenic world. The hegemony in Greece and the leadership in maritime affairs passed from Sparta to her. She organized the Confederacy of Delos, later used the "dues" of the Delian League to strengthen her own navy and gradually reduced nearly all her allies to a state of vassalage; her armaments increased enormously and the dues contributed by the members of the League were a virtual subsidy to Athens to protect them. It was upon this pretext at least that Pericles, when he came to power, transferred the treasury of the League bodily to Athens and used the funds in his projects for beautifying the city and the restoration of the fanes the Persians had destroyed.

At certain epochs in the history of the world, conditions and events seem to conspire to produce great men and great works; as in favored corners of the Gallic vineyards the soil yields a wine of special excellence, so at this time in this happy-starred Attica the Greek spirit had its richest vintage; and the Golden Age of Athenian literature inaugurated in this period was destined to outlast the supremacy of the other arts of Athens and continue far into the Alexandrian Age. Chief among the amazing galaxy of artistic personalities of the Pericleian Age was Phidias, born at Athens in 490 B. C., the year of the battle of Marathon. His teachers were said to have been Hegias of Attica, and Ageladas, the foremost figure of the Argive school of sculpture. He became the Director of Works for Pericles. The pediment figures and the frieze of the Parthenon were his; all of the former that survived the ravages of time, the Turk, and the Venetians, were taken, with part of the frieze, by Lord Elgin to London, where, as the Elgin Marbles, they are to be seen in the British Museum. The chryselephantine statue of Olympian Zeus at Olympia in Elis was his also, and he maintained a studio or workshop at that focus of Hellenic life. Phidias was the author of thirteen bronze figures dedicated at Delphi by the Athenians out of the booty from the battle of Marathon; for steel was unknown, and weapons, shields, and armor, were of hardened bronze, readily converted into statuary. His bronze colossus of Athene Promachos, erected on the Athenian Acropolis to celebrate the victory over the Persians, towered above the temples themselves; and the sun could be seen glinting on her spear-tip by mariners rounding the headland of Sunium fifty miles away. He was prosecuted on a charge of sacrilege trumped up by the personal and political enemies of his friend and patron Pericles for having introduced portraits of himself and his chief on the shield of the statue of Athene Parthenos, the Virgin Athena, in her temple the Parthenon, and is said to have died in prison! His work marks the transition from the primitive or archaic manner to the fully developed style of Attica.

Ictinus, the architect of the Parthenon, was presumably an Athenian, but the exact dates of the birth and death of this man who was one of the most exquisitely gifted artists of all time are unknown. He was the author of the Temple of the Mysteries at Eleusis in Attica, and of the temple of Apollo Epicurius—the ally or helper—at Bassæ up in the grey hills near Phigalia in Arcadia, erected by the Arcadians to Apollo in gratitude for the deliverance of Arcadia from the same plague that devastated Athens and of which Pericles sickened and died. With Ictinus on the Parthenon was associated that Callicrates who was the architect of the tiny Temple of Niké Apteros at the gates of the Acropolis of Athens.

Polyclitus, sculptor and architect, was a native of Argolis

and the recognized head of the school of sculpture of Argos and Sicyon, renowned for proficiency in the casting of bronze statues; his Doryphoros or Spear Bearer was called "The Rule" because of its perfections. Among other works he made the chryselephantine statue of Hera at Argos, the centre of the national worship of Hera.

Myron the Athenian was another great sculptor, whose Standing Discobolus or Thrower of the Discus, and Stooping Discobolus, are famous. The latter illustrates to a marvel what has been said of arrested action and equilibrium in sculpture; Myron chose the exact fraction of a second when the downward sweep of the arm has ended and the upward throw has not yet begun.

Polygnotus, the painter, was a native of the island of Thasos, and came of a family of painters; he was known as the Prometheus of painting from the vigor of his work. He would accept no pay but received honors at Delphi and citizenship in Athens. His most celebrated works were two great paintings on the walls of a Stoa, or covered and colonnaded public promenade, at Delphi in Phocis, representing Hades and the Fall of Troy. He also painted the Stoa Poekile or Echo Colonnade at Athens, built by Peixianax the brother-in-law of Cimon, who was the rival of Pericles, and probably decorated other Athenian buildings. A younger contemporary of Polygnotus, and apparently more popular than he, was Micon, an Athenian, sculptor as well as painter. He painted the fabled contests of the Athenians with the Amazons, and scenes from the life of Theseus. In partnership with Panænus he executed a picture of the battle of Marathon, well-known in its time. Zeuxis and Agatharcus were other celebrated painters, unfortunate like their fellows in the complete destruction of their works.

Mnesicles was the architect of the Propylæa and the

Erechtheum. His most fruitful years were those from 437 to about 415 B. C. but the time and even the place of birth of this great artist are unknown.

The latter part of this period of prosperity, comparative peace, and consequent artistic accomplishment, was darkened by the death of Pericles in 429 and by the struggle for supremacy between Athens and Sparta—the Peloponnesian War—involving all the states and cities of Hellas until 404. But it was illumined by the birth of Plato the philosopher, born in the year of Pericles' death. We are not accustomed to associate the qualities of the man of action with those of the philosopher; nor do we associate Socrates, the teacher of Plato, with battles and the strenuous life—and yet he fought bravely at the side of another pupil, the young Alcibiades, in some of the wars of Attica; but this was entirely characteristic of Greek custom; every citizen bore his share in the civil and military burdens of the state. So Plato, thus called from the breadth of his shoulders, the son of Ariston, a famous athlete, won victories in wrestling at the Pythian games at Delphi and at the Nemean and the Isthmian games. While a guest of Dionysius I, Tyrant of Syracuse, he offended his host, who caused him to be sold as a slave. Plato was ransomed by a friend. This adventure in Sicily, the imprisonment of Phidias already referred to, and the fate of Plato's master Socrates, condemned to drink the poison distilled from hemlock, seem to indicate that even at this time of enlightenment the life of the intellectual man was subject to hazard. Indeed, it is clear from what Mahaffy says that the extremes of savagery and brutality were co-existent with artistic and intellectual refinement throughout the world of Hellas and envy and jealousy played their parts as prominent traits in the Greek nature.

The Age of Pericles lighted the paths of men for many a

golden year. But it is not by the reflected light of those sixty wondrous years that such men as Praxiteles and his contemporaries shone. The work of the years following the death of Pericles should be regarded rather as the natural sequel of the Golden Age, the natural reaction to its tremendous stimuli. The architect Hippodamus of Miletus in Caria, Asia Minor, planned the Piræus, the port of Athens, and laid out the city of Rhodes, which, later, in the Alexandrian Age, became one of the chief centres of Greek art. To Callimachus, architect and sculptor, is ascribed the invention of the Corinthian capital in a pretty legend about as sound when examined in the light of qualified criticism as the myth that the arches of the Gothic cathedrals reproduce the aisles of the forests with their overarching branches. One of the leading artists of this period was Scopas, both architect and sculptor, active in Ionia and in Caria, and one of the sculptors employed by Artemisia, Queen of Caria and widow of Mausolus, upon the tomb she built for her husband and which has given a generic name to all such mortuary buildings—the Mausoleum at Halicarnassus, and of which the architects were Satyrus and Pythius. Scopas also carved one of the plinths of the columns of the Temple of Diana at Ephesus; and the famous group representing Niobe and her Children is also ascribed to him.

The name of Praxiteles gives its chief lustre to this second blossoming of the Greek genius; he came of a line of Athenian sculptors, his grandfather of the same name having been celebrated in the fifth century. His father was Cephisodotus, who made the group of Eirene with the child Plutus in her arms. Praxiteles was older than but a contemporary of Lysippus, of the bronze school of Argos and Sicyon. He was the author of the Cnidian Aphrodite, the so-called Venus de' Medici, which stood in the Temple of Aphrodite on

Cnidus, an Ionian isle. The beautiful Hermes with the Infant Dionysus in his arms, found about the middle of the nineteenth century lying on its face where it had fallen in the ashes of the roof of the Temple of Hera at Olympia in Elis, was his. He had a son named after his father Cephisodotus, who was his artistic heir; another son was Timarchus, and the statue of Menander which stood in the Theatre of Dionysus at Athens was the joint work of these brothers.

Lysippus, to whom reference has been made, was a native of Sicyon in the Peloponnesus, and is said to have produced some fifteen hundred works, among them Kairos, or Passing Opportunity; the Apoxyonemos; a portrait of Alexander the Great; and one of Sophocles.

Apelles, one of the great names in painting that have come down to us, was a native of Colophon in Lydia, Asia Minor. Besides portraits of Alexander, he painted Calumny; Artemis surrounded by her Nymphs; Aphrodite Anadyomene or Venus rising from the Sea; and many other things, all of which have perished and of which only vague and unsatisfactory descriptions survive. But they are mentioned here to indicate that a new order of subject was being treated by the artist, such as the "Passing Opportunity" of Lysippus and the "Calumny" of Apelles, and a broadening of the artistic horizon as well as increased power and technical resources to render subjects of a psychological character.

Toward the close of the post-Pericleian period, or about 340 B. C., the Theatre of Dionysus at Athens, used also as the usual place of public assembly, was built by an unknown architect on the side of the Acropolis facing toward Phaleron and the sea. The Greeks usually selected sites for their theatres on the flanks of hills where the conformation of the ground gave a natural amphitheatre so that there should be the minimum of excavation or of construction, and such hillside slopes almost always in Greece command beautiful views of sea and headland or distant island. But this prospect was always screened from the view of the audience by a cloth or wooden "scena," which became later, in the Roman theatre, a high wall of stone frequently treated with much architectural elaboration. Thus vanishes the myth that the view served in lieu of painted scenery. Nothing could be more distracting during a theatrical performance than a great natural panorama behind the actors, leading the mind away from the stage and the play. Nor could the persons or the passions of human beings fail to seem small and trivial in a setting of such stupendous scale.

CHAPTER XII

THE ALEXANDRIAN AGE AND THE GREEK DECLINE

The Third Period of Grecian Art — Alexander the Great — Alexandria Founded — The Stadium at Athens — The Choragic Monument of Lysicrates — The Partition of Alexander's Empire — The Ptolemies — Decline of Athenian Supremacy in the Arts — Rise of Rhodes and Pergamum as Artistic Centres — Rhodian Sculpture — The Olympic Festivals — The Delphic Oracle — The Romans and Their Rise to Power — Greece Becomes a Roman Province.

WHILE the work of building the immense Theatre of Dionysus was still going on in Athens, Philip of Macedon passed Thermopylæ in 338 B. C., established the dominion of Macedon over Greece, was assassinated two years later, and was succeeded by his son, the pupil of Aristotle the philosopher, Alexander the Great. This young man, who reigned from 336 to 323 B. C., in these thirteen years conquered Egypt, part of North Africa, Syria, Asia Minor, Persia, and India as far as the Indus. He planned to Hellenize the world and indeed did more in his short lease of power to spread Hellenic culture in the East than years of peaceful penetration would have accomplished. His reign inaugurates the third period of Grecian art, the Alexandrian Age, in which the centre of learning and culture was to shift to the city he founded in the Nile Delta and bestowed his name upon—the city of Alexandria.

During his rule was built the Athenian Stadium, where the athletic contests were held. Also the Temple of Diana at Ephesus in Lydia; this was the third structure; the second was set on fire the night Alexander was born. It was one of the wonders of the then known world, and assumed the character of a great national gallery of painting and sculpture and the value of the votive offerings was beyond all computation. Pæonius and Demetrius of Ephesus were the architects.

In a quiet corner of Athens there stands a little structure erected in the year following Alexander's accession, known as the Choragic Monument of Lysicrates; it is the only surviving example of one of the forms given to a base or pedestal for the exhibition of the bronze tripod offered as the prize at the Dionysiac Festivals in Athens; this monument and the care lavished upon it is a bare intimation of the importance such an event as that which it celebrated held in Athenian eyes; and this is but a lone survivor of a long street of such monuments extending from the theatre to the town. Its author is unknown. The inscription brings a vivid series of pictures before us; it reads: "Lysikrates, son of Lysitheiedes of Kikyuna, was Choragos when the boy-chorus of the Phyle Akamantis won the prize. Theon was the flute player, Lysiades of Athens trained the chorus. Enænetos was Archon."

After Alexander died at Babylon, by the close of the century his power and his dominions were partitioned among those who had been his generals; to Cassander ultimately fell Macedonia and Greece; to Lysimachus, Thrace and the western part of Asia Minor; to Seleucus Nicator, Syria, and easterly to the Indus. To Ptolemy Logi, founder of the Ptolemaic dynasty, Egypt was apportioned; here he ruled as governor till 306 and as King from then until his death in 285 B. C. He founded the famous Museum in Alexandria containing the Alexandrian Library, which was burned by the Moslems, the resort of savants from all lands. His aim and that of his son, Ptolemy Philadelphus, was to make

Alexandria the intellectual centre of the world. Among other works he ordered the construction of the Pharos, the lighthouse of the port of Alexandria, reckoned as one of the ancient Seven Wonders. Soon after the partition of Alexander's empire quarrels arose among the successors which extended with the various concomitants of wars, raids, sacks, and assassinations over many years. Ptolemy, favored by distance, succeeded in keeping himself fairly aloof from these broils, and during his long and peaceful reign and that of his son the arts of peace flourished in Egypt.

Athens was no longer supreme in the arts. Among others, the city of Rhodes became a great artistic centre; also Pergamum in Asia Minor. The Rhodian School was renowned for sculpture; the Colossus of Rhodes, another of the Seven Wonders, was only one of many colossi erected there. This one in particular was the work of the sculptor Chares and was built from metal parts of war engines designed and used by Demetrius Poliorcetes, called the Besieger, in his unsuccessful siege of Rhodes and which the Rhodians begged of him as a memorial of his military genius, despite his nonsuccess. The Laocoön in the Vatican, and the Farnese Bull or Toro Farnese, by Apollonius and Tauriscus of Tralles, brought to Rome in the time of Augustus, discovered in the ruins of the Baths of Caracalla, and now in the Naples Museum, are two examples of Rhodian sculpture. This Demetrius Poliorcetes, son of Antigonus of Macedon, won a naval victory over Ptolemy in 306 B. C. and as a memorial set up in Samothrace, the island off which the battle was fought, the beautiful Niké or Winged Victory now enshrined in the Louvre in Paris with the Venus of Milo, the Aphrodite found in the Island of Melos in 1820. How many masterpieces of this and other periods have been destroyed, who may say ? Of all the glorious company that made the ways

THE WINGED VICTORY OF SAMOTHRACE, erected by Demetrius Poliorcetes (Demetrius the Besieger) in the Island of Samothrace to celebrate his naval victory over Ptolemy of Egypt in 306 B. C., therefore a work of the Early Alexandrian Age. Victory is represented as having alighted upon the prow of a galley which forms the pedestal. Even in its mutilated condition, the sweep and flutter of the robes in the wind make it one of the most thrilling relics of Grecian art.

of men beautiful and good to linger in, so few, so very few have survived.

No survey of Greek culture however brief may fail of reference to the national shrines at Olympia in Elis nor to the Oracles, especially to that at Delphi. Olympia had early become the national meeting ground for all the Hellenes, and every four years they dropped their wars, raids, piracies, and squabbles, declared a sacred truce and repaired to Olympia to contend with each other in athletics, poetry, and music. The prize was a simple wreath of laurel. These Olympic games as well as the Nemean, Isthmian, and Pythian games, came to have a large influence upon Greek art, for victors either had their statues erected by their proud cities or, failing this, with exquisite modesty set them up themselves. All the cities of Greece constructed buildings at Olympia. The votive offerings in the temples, objects in gold and silver, presented by the cities as propitiatory or thank offerings to the gods, were rich beyond measure. This was the place where artists not only exhibited their works and gained a national reputation, but measured their powers against others; so that the Olympic festivals were a constantly renewed stimulus to all the arts of design.

At Delphi in Phocis there is a valley in the flank of the mountains that sweep backward to Parnassus, and in the midst of the valley a cleft in the rock whence issued gaseous vapors that made goats behave strangely and caused men to fall to prophecy. A Sacred Python was believed to dwell in the cavern and it was his sacred gaseous breath which appeared in these vapors. Apollo having slain the Python—whose breath kept on regardless, it would seem—this lovely valley became the shrine of Apollo and a temple was erected to him. Here dwelt the Priestess of the Oracle of Delphi and to the Oracle kings and cities, not merely of the Greek world, submitted questions of state and policy. It was a national shrine and a sort of national museum like the Temple of Artemis at Ephesus. In 548 B. C. the temple was burned and all the states and cities of Hellas contributed to its reconstruction. The temple itself and the buildings erected as treasuries by the Hellenes were crammed with the spoils of many battle-fields, rich gifts of rulers, and rare works of art. The Phocians, in whose province it stood, later despoiled it of a treasure valued in millions and the Romans stripped it bare of the artistic treasures the Phocians left behind.

We must reckon with these Romans now. The power of Rome had been steadily growing. Little by little she had extended her domain, destroyed the ancient Etruscan civilization in Central Italy, conquered the greater part of the Italian peninsula, and then, forced to it by the menace of Carthage which was colonizing in Sicily and ravaging the Hellenic cities there at the very gates of Rome, she became a maritime power also, deleted Carthage after three long and devastating wars, and entered upon the conquest of the world. During the course of the second war with Carthage, known as the Second Punic War and which lasted from 219 to 201 B. C., she became involved in a conflict with Philip V of Macedon whose alliance the Carthaginians had sought. She had already, in punishing the Illyrian corsairs who infested the Adriatic, assumed a kind of protectorate over the Greek cities on the Adriatic, the first step to supremacy in Greece and all the East. After a series of wars and declarations of peace, Rome, in 197 B. C. through her general Flaminius, proclaimed the freedom of Greece. But Antiochus the Great of Syria, having allied himself with the Ætolian League, a confederacy of certain Greek cities, took up arms against Rome. He thus needlessly drew the Romans into

A little FLYING VICTORY in bronze, from Pompeii, now in the Naples Museum, and originally suspended from a ceiling, the ball being a modern addition. It is an intimation of the incredible wealth of antiquity in works of art.

Statuette of a NARCISSUS (or Dionysus) of the School of Praxiteles, possibly a copy of some celebrated statue, rescued from the ruins of Pompeii, now in Naples. The attitude would suggest some adjunct now missing, such as a kid or panther.

Head and Torso of PSYCHE, in the Naples Museum, a Greek fragment found at Capua, just north of Naples, once a very important town. Hundreds of exquisite things like this must have perished during disturbances such as the Barbarian invasions.

FAUN WITH YOUNG BACCHUS, in the Naples Museum. A Roman or Græco-Roman work in marble. A marble bar has been left between the lower legs to strengthen them, and the tree stump is introduced for the same purpose.

Asia; by uniting with Madedon and Carthage he could have carried the war into Italy and prevented the spread of the Roman power. Scipio Africanus vanquished Antiochus, forced him to relinquish the greater part of Asia Minor and annexed it to the domain of Attalus, King of Pergamum, an enlightened patron of arts and letters, an ally of Rome, and whose successor, Attalus III, bequeathed his whole kingdom to the Roman people. The end was not far off. Macedon was subjugated at last, and the Achæan League, another Greek confederacy, went down before the Romans under Mummius, who destroyed Corinth and sent off shiploads of works of art to Rome, although during the sack great numbers of wonderful things had perished; and the ignorant Roman legionaries, recruited from all parts of the world, used priceless paintings for dice-boards or trampled them under their brutal feet.

As a Roman province under the name of Achæa the Greece we have described disappears from history like a tale that is told. Theatre and fane, column and wall, have crumbled into dust. Man, more ruthless than the elements, in violence and greed, in ignorance and sloth, defacing, despoiling, neglecting, has done more than they to ruin or destroy. Yet Hellas, smiling in her broken beauty down the ages, has leavened all the world; and through the ferric clangor of this later age, in the inner ear of those who love her, still sound the golden bells of Greece.

CHAPTER XIII

ROME AND THE ROMANS

The Italian Peninsula — The Italian Tribes — The Beauty of Their Fertile Land — The Foundation of Rome — The Roman Genius in Administration and in Building — The Greek and the Roman Compared — The Kings and the Republic — Civic Virtue — Emergence of Personalities — Permeation of Roman Society by Hellenic Culture — The Birth of the Roman Empire — Its Structures — Their Wide-spread Distribution — Roman Law, Civilization, and Building, Become the Universal Type.

THE Italian peninsula, like the Hellenic, is so modelled, so subdivided by natural mountainous barriers that as in Greece there could be, under living conditions in primitive times, no national life in the sense in which we understand that term to-day; nor until late in the nineteenth century when science had conquered these physical barriers did Italy achieve national unity in the modern sense. Separated though they were, the peoples who called themselves Hellenes had a strong sense of racial unity. But the tribes which pursued their rude agriculture and grazed their flocks and herds under Italian skies felt no such bond. The apparent unity under Roman rule was a unity imposed by force upon innumerable tribal communities of alien types and origins welded together by the Roman fist.

Never was a land more fertile or more fair. Magnificent mountain ranges, lakes of incredible loveliness, plains for tillage or for pasture, hillsides for the culture of the olive, the grape, and the most luscious fruits of earth, dowered with a soft and kindly climate, bounded on every side save the north by the amethystine waters of warm inland seas— never has there been a land more loved, more coveted, more drenched with blood, more fertile of beauty. The Apennine chain, running diagonally across the peninsula, sweeps southward to form the precipitous easterly coast which combines with the marshy shores of the Emilia farther north to make the eastern littoral unfriendly and inhospitable. The greater part of Italy therefore faces the west and Mommsen has pointed out that since Greece faces east the two countries turn their backs upon each other, and he accounts in this way for the lack of direct relations between Rome and the cities of Greece for many centuries.

At a fordable place on the River Tiber marked by seven low hills the future city of Rome was founded by a band of landless, masterless men, half brigands, half herdsmen or shepherds. To the north and northwest of this place lay Etruria, the seat of a race of uncertain origin and from whom the rude denizens of the huddle of huts by the Tiber learned much of religion, of the art of building, and of the elements of civilized life, and whose civilization, akin in many ways to that of the Greek colonists in Magna Græcia, the Romans later utterly destroyed.

The genius of the race the Romans slowly hammered together was essentially practical, constructive, executive, military. Whereas, Hegel says, the Greeks and the peoples farther east embody the poetry of the human spirit, in the Romans we find its prose. If they had the genius of conquest they possessed also the gift of governing their conquests with a justice harsh and stern but salutary to the semi-barbarous folk they dealt with. In her early days and indeed almost throughout her history, in spite of instances of wholesale deportations from the provinces beyond Italy, Rome, instead of wiping out conquered peoples and obliterating their places of abode, incorporated them with her body politic, gradually extending Roman citizenship until nearly all the peninsula participated in its rights and benefits. Wherever she went she brought order under the law, instituting public works of utility, water-supply and sewage systems, great roads paved with stone from curb to curb and patrolled, policed, and made safe for men to use.

We must not fail to note that both the Roman and the Greek worlds were, as were all ancient civilizations, stained with what we moderns regard as the crime of slavery. The social fabric of Greece could not have existed in the forms it assumed without it. The Roman cities swarmed with slaves from every corner of the civilized and uncivilized earth. Slave labor gave time and wealth for many things that could not be afforded under a system of paid labor. The conditions varied of course according to the people and the master. Slavery was no respecter of persons; it brought the highest and the lowest born, the savage and the sage, to one level of servitude to alien masters.

It has been the fashion to sneer at the Roman as a vulgarian from whom the things of beauty were sealed away. No doubt the Roman populace had no such appreciation of art as that ascribed to the Athenian. No doubt the Roman architect lacked that exquisite sense of form and the gift for the evocation of beautiful detail possessed by the Greek; but in constructive genius the Roman far surpassed him. Although the same sources were open to the Greek as those from which the Roman evolved his stupendous vaults, airy domes, and majestic arches, it never seems to have occurred to the Greek that here were new founts of beauty to be drawn upon—therefore I say that the constructive sense was keener in the Roman. The hypothesis that the Greeks deliberately ignored the arch, the vault, and the dome, in favor of what they deemed a higher beauty is unsound; they merely lacked a broad sense of the possibilities

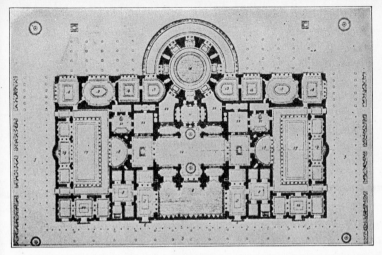

*PLAN OF THE BATHS OF THE EMPEROR CARACALLA, built in Rome about
212 A. D. In the scientific arrangement and relations of the many rooms and spaces, in their
balance and symmetry, in the grouping of the smaller about the larger which rise above them,
in the provisions for light and air, and in all that contributes to majesty and convenience in
architecture, this building and those like it are the source of the modern science of plan.*

*THE ROMAN FORUM, from the cyclorama by Bühlmann, in which the Rome of Con-
stantine is shown as it appeared in 312 A. D. The open space in the centre, through which
the procession is seen following the course of the Sacred Way, is the Forum proper. The
little circular temple on the right side is the Temple of Vesta, the hearth of the Roman people, just under the Palace of the Cæsars. In the left distance, the huge bulk of the Colosseum.*

in building construction. The Roman developed the science of plan and found means to cover over vast spaces with imposing majesty; the germ of the whole science of planning as practised to-day may be found in the Baths of Caracalla. He invented and evolved new types of buildings to suit new conditions of public or of private use; he threw huge bridges which endure to this moment over roaring rivers, and brought the pure waters of the hills across great reaches of hill and campagna to refresh his cities and supply the baths and the fountains in the public places. The genius of Rome was for architecture, as the genius of Greece was supremely for sculpture, and as we shall find the genius of the Italians of the Renaissance to be eminently for painting.

From the reputed foundation of the city in 753 B. C., twenty-three years after the first Olympic festival, to the expulsion of the Etruscan Tarquins in 510, Rome was under the rule of kings. Of this period nothing of an artistic nature remains, but we hear of such public works as the Cloaca Maxima, the trunk sewer of Rome, and the city walls and certain temples vanished long ago. Rome became a republic when the last of the Tarquins was cast out; ensued a long period of gradual expansion and of conquest in her immediate neighborhood—a period, too, of civic and indeed of personal virtue, a surrender of self in the service of the state for the good of all, that would be remarkable at any time in the world's history. During this long tale of years the annals of Rome are chronicles of laws worked out, of civic problems solved, of administrative systems evolved, of military science perfected, punctuated by the appearance of the Northern peoples in 388 B. C. when the Gauls under Brennus overran Italy and burned Rome itself, but mute as to public works of art until the Appian Way was built by Claudius Appius and later the Aqueduct known by his name. Sicily with all its heritage of Hellenic culture and tradition fell under her sway in the mid years of the third century before Christ and now began the wars with Carthage which led her beyond the Italian peninsula and to the ultimate domination of the world through the destruction of that old Phœnician stronghold, the extinction of Macedon, and the protectorate of Greece. During the earlier years of the Republic, while this or that head shows occasionally above the crowd, the individual was submerged in the Citizen of Rome; but toward its close, contributing of course to its fall but developing as a natural effect of conditions, personalities are emergent, like the Scipios and the Gracchi; Marius; Julius Cæsar and Sulla and Pompey. As the civic virtue of the Roman Republic declined, the Republic decayed with it as an inevitable sequel. The Mediterranean world was in a state of chaos. Without political stability and a state of peace the arts cannot develop. The time was ripe for the strong hands of the Cæsars to take the reins and bring order to the world, uniformity of law and of custom.

During all the Alexandrian period the patricians of Rome looked to Greece and particularly to that Athens which was still revered as the authentic fount of culture. They engaged Greek tutors for their sons, if they had not already learned Greek slaves in their households, or sent their youth to Athens or to Alexandria to be instructed. Thus, and by the close contact with the Hellenic civilizations of Magna Græcia and Sicily as well as by wholesale deportations of Hellenes to Rome, Roman society came to be permeated by Greek culture, ameliorating the mental life of the better classes, and preparing the way for the magnificence of the Empire and the consequent employment of great numbers of Greek artists and artisans upon the vast artistic enterprises decreed by the Cæsars.

Mahaffy thinks there was an amiable weakness in the policy of Rome toward Greece which arose from the desire to appear cultivated and from the anxiety to rank as descendants of Æneas and colonists from Ilium. This was apparently not incompatible with a rapacity that carried off the gathered artistic treasures of centuries from conquered cities leaving them stripped to the bare stones, nor with the policy which, during the decadent years of the Republic, deprived whole countries of their best blood and brains by the series of wholesale deportations referred to. Nor, such are the contradictions as between personal and national morality, did it affect the fact that the probity of the Roman was far greater than that of the Greek. Hear Polybius, the Greek historian, on this point: "Public men among the Greeks, if they be trusted with but one talent, though you take ten copies of the deed and affix two seals and have twenty witnesses, cannot keep their trust, whereas among the Romans, though handling great sums in their offices and embassies, men hold to their duty under the simple bond of an oath. Elsewhere it is hard to find a man keeping his hands off public money, and pure in this respect; at Rome it is hard to find a man guilty of such conduct." Polybius comments also upon the corruption of the Roman patrician society by the license of the Greeks, themselves perverted by contact with the decadent morals of Asia.

It is credible that after the Romans came into close contact with Grecian culture, after the problems of consolidating and governing their fast-growing empire had been solved, and particularly after the flood of works of art from all parts of the world had set in, they began to appreciate, at least as intelligently as the average patron of art, the high office of art in the world. I believe it to be most probable, because it is always the way in periods of transition, that the Roman architect designed and planned his structures in their general features and employed the Greek artist or artisan in their embellishment. But after long residence in Italy, after the intermarriages and social adjustments of successive generations, the Greek artist must have been completely absorbed. One thing is certain—the grand traits of Roman work are Roman; it is only in minor details that we encounter the refinements we may ascribe to a Greek hand. I am referring of course to architecture. Painting is the most perishable of the arts and of Roman painting we have few traces and those are of a purely decorative sort. What sculpture there was of an original nature was probably done by resident Greeks; there was a thriving trade in reproductions of famous Greek sculptures, and at a certain period a curious reversion to the archaic type, quite like a similar affectation of the present moment in America; this work is known as archaistic; the whole movement, including the reproduction of antique sculpture is analagous to that rage for antiques which seizes every parvenu and non-creative society.

The several steps by which Julius Cæsar rose to prominence, conquered new provinces for Rome, was made Dictator for life and was assassinated by Brutus and Cassius and a band of envious conspirators need not detain us here, nor those by which Octavius Cæsar, his nephew, became master of the world and the first Roman Emperor. It is said of this Augustus that he found Rome brick and left her in marble; but the authors of the many vast structures of the Roman Empire are unknown—a significant indication of the probable status of the artist. The list of Roman remains represents not a thousandth part of what was done in the years between the assumption of the purple by Augustus and the removal of the capital of the Empire to Byzantium

The *CASTLE OF S. ANGELO, in Rome,*
originally the Mausoleum of the Emperor
Hadrian and perhaps then surmounted by a
conical mound of earth planted with trees
and shrubs. For many years a fortress, the
battlements are Mediæval alterations.

The *PONT–DU–GARD, near Nîmes,*
France, spanning the River Gard, about 900
feet long and 180 above the river. Part of a
Roman aqueduct nearly 25 miles long. One
of the splendid civic structures of the Romans,
built about 19 B. C.

The *TRIUMPHAL ARCH built for the Emperor CONSTANTINE in Rome by an un-*
known architect after 306 A. D., at a time of sculptural and architectural decadence. The sculp-
tures on this arch were taken from other structures, and possibly the columns and other details
also. The general form and character, however, are typical of this class of Roman monument,
the central arch serving for chariots, the side arches for pedestrians. The prototype of mod-
ern arches, such as the Arc du Carrousel in Paris.

by Constantine in 330 A. D. There were arches, bridges, aqueducts, vast harbors surrounded by quays and warehouses of stone, immense public baths, basilicas (law courts which are the prototype of the Christian church), amphitheatres, circuses, theatres, villas, fora, everywhere. A forum was a public square of meeting place for debate on public questions, for voting, and for lounging and loafing; several of the Emperors, Trajan and Vespasian among them, built fora to curry and keep the favor of the populace. There was a forum where cattle was sold. These are not to be confused with the Forum Romanum, the great Forum of Rome, which grew naturally and not as the result of Imperial fiat and which, surrounded by large structures set on inadequate sites at all sorts of angles and crowded with statues, rostral columns and trophies, altars, rostra, and polling places, must have presented an appearance quite at variance with those ideas of classical symmetry which are, with other myths, part of our legacy from that fount of inaccurate impressions, the Victorian era.

Every provincial city strove to be a Rome in miniature. Every Roman official sought to create about him the atmosphere and the material comforts of the metropolis. The Roman organization, the Roman governmental system, resulted in the distribution throughout the world of the Roman type of law, of daily custom, and of the arts of design. On the eve of the fall of the Roman Empire and the Dark Ages that supervened, the work of Roman hands throughout the world was like a cache of precious things buried against impending calamity, to be exhumed in better days; and it was to this that the later builders were to turn for the inspiration that led them on to the marvels of the Gothic and the splendors of the Renaissance.

CHAPTER XIV

THE FIRST MILLENNIUM OF THE CHRISTIAN ERA

The Religion of Christ — The Basilicas as Christian Churches — Byzantium, renamed Constantinople, the new Capital of the World — The Byzantine Style — The Germanic Barbarians — The Empire of the West Disappears — The Results of the Barbarian Irruptions — Mohammed and his new Faith — The Moslem Civilization — Its Effect upon Architecture — Charlemagne — The Norsemen — The Norman Type of Romanesque — The First Millennium — The Crusades.

THE religion of Christ, which had been furtively practised for three centuries, and its devotees, principally members of the humbler classes, persecuted, had gathered strength, and its doctrines had invaded the palaces of the patricians; by the time of Constantine its status was such that he could first proclaim it to be on an equal footing with the other faiths of the Empire and subsequently make it the state religion. The Christian congregations, when they were free to venture forth from the catacombs and other secret places of their worship, were first allowed to use the basilicas, or law courts, many of them fallen into disuse in Italy through the removal of the seat of government to Byzantium. From the simple germ of the basilican plan were gradually evolved the rich and splendid plans of the cathedrals of the Middle Ages.

In his new capital of Constantinople, to which Constantine had summoned the artists of the Empire to make the re-christened city of Byzantium worthy of the glory of the Roman name, there developed, out of the conditions of its site on the Golden Horn, equally in touch with Greece and

AYA SOFIA, the Church of the Divine Wisdom, built in Constantinople under the auspices of Justinian, Emperor of the East, A. D. 532, comparable in dimension with St. Paul's, London, the domes being respectively 107 and 109 feet in diameter. It is now a Turkish mosque, and the decorations were for centuries obscured by whitewash laid on by the devout Mohammedans. It is a Byzantine structure of the purest type and had a powerful influence upon all Byzantine and much Romanesque design.

The BASILICA DI SAN MARCO, Venice, an extraordinary melange of architectural styles. Begun in 830 A. D., reconstructed in the eleventh century in the Byzantine manner, with additions of Gothic detail in the fifteenth century, and mosaics of a still later date, the Venetians, always in intimate contact with the Levant, lavished riches of Eastern marbles and mosaics upon this, their greatest treasure. The curious domes covered with lead are Saracenic in character. Here the Doges were crowned and stately festivals held.

the arts of the farther East, a new and luxuriant style known as the Byzantine, combining many evidences of the influence of Greek art in its carved details, a superb use of color due to Asian sources of inspiration, and the traditions of Rome in arch and vault and the use of rich marbles. The new style spread through the channels of trade and of national intercourse; it reacted upon the city of Rome itself and produced many of the Christian basilicas—the first churches built by the Christians on the general plan of the secular basilicas. We have here to record the regrettable fact that the early Christians through ignorance and misguided religious zeal are responsible both in Greece and Italy for the destruction of many of the beautiful monuments of antiquity, stealing the marble columns, using the walls as quarries or defacing them to dig out the metal clamps, and burning the most exquisite marble sculptures for the lime. It is but fair to say that vandalism of this sort was rife for centuries—indeed until quite recent years.

Not long after the new seat of empire had been established, there occurred one of those strange episodes in the history of mankind that have grave and far-reaching issues—the movement of the Barbarians. We have already noted their earlier descents upon the civilized lands to the south of them. But those we have now to record were far more serious and their sequels in the ethnical, political, and artistic worlds, important. The Visigoths and the Ostrogoths—the Western and the Eastern Goths—whose very name had become a terror to the southlands and who had been held beyond the Danube, sued for permission to cross the river and place it between them and a horde more terrible than they had ever been—the Huns, who were sweeping westward in an irresistible wave. Once across, they began their usual course of plunder and rapine; and the Visigoths under Alaric sacked Rome in 410 A. D. for six days and nights. Not long afterward the Vandals, more dreaded than the Goths, passing through Spain and North Africa, plundering, burning, massacring as they went, invaded Sicily from the vantage ground of Tunis, reached Rome under Genseric and sacked it in their turn. Then came Attila with his Huns, who made it his boast that the grass never grew again where once his horse's hoof had trod. He was decisively defeated in 451 and with his defeat was determined the question whether Europe was to be heathen or Christian. The survivors of these waves of invasion, those neither killed nor enslaved, either retired to their native steppes and forests in Russia and Germany or were absorbed into the populations of the lands they had ravaged and pillaged.

The fabric of the Roman Empire was shaken by the fury of these onslaughts and in 476 the Empire of the West ceased to be and Italy became a province of the Empire of the East. The complete removal of secular authority from Rome was a strongly contributing cause of the growth of power of the Bishops of the Church of Rome, soon to become a new world force as the Papacy.

The desolation, devastation, and misery wrought by the Barbarians, added to the horrors of successive epidemics that dealt death to vast numbers of persons, had a frightful effect upon all the arts. There was no longer any education nor means of obtaining it, and ignorance the most appalling descended like a sable cloud upon the masses of the people. What vestiges of learning there were took refuge with men of letters in the monasteries that began to spring up in Europe. As if Hun, Vandal, and pestilence were not enough, Leo, the Isaurian, the Emperor at Byzantium, embraced the Heresy of the Iconoclasts so-called, and persecuted with fury all those engaged in the pursuits of art or learning.

The common people in Italy, in the provinces of Gaul, and elsewhere forgot their old traditions, lost the memory of their past completely, and at last believed the work of their own ancestors to be that of magicians and potent sorcerers. Only in Constantinople, whose name reverted to the original Byzantium, did there burn some of the authentic fire of the arts. However, these five frightful centuries between the fifth and the tenth were necessary for worn and decadent Italy in which to absorb the infusion of strong, fresh Northern blood she had received, assimilate the new elements, and gather strength for future tasks.

In the meantime, while the Christianized world of the West was sunk in a deathlike stupor, an Arabian camel-driver and trader named Mohammed, down in Mecca in the Arabian desert, invented for himself a new religion and declared himself the Prophet of it. It was based in some particulars upon the same ideas as the Jewish belief, was suited to the simple desert peoples, and its tenets were stated with precision; it professed one God; it provided four wives for every man who could provide for them—a popular provision; and the point that is of special interest to the student of art is that it adopted literally and applied rigorously the Mosaic commandment as to graven images and banished the representation of any living thing, man, beast, bird, fish, or vegetable from Mohammedan art. To this prohibition is due its distinctive character, which depends for all the decorative elements of design upon the most ingenious and intricate arrangements and interlacements of lines and bands decorated with vivid and beautiful color.

In five and twenty years the new faith had been spread by the Moslem sword along the North African littoral, overwhelmed Persia, extended nearly to the Indus and up to the Oxus and the Caspian Sea. In another hundred years all of North Africa including Egypt, all of Spain, the East beyond the Indus, and most of Turkestan were under Moslem rule. Then its advance slackened until the Turks, new converts to the faith of Islam, poured down out of the mountains of Turkestan and, adding Asia Minor to the Company of the Faithful, revived the intense and fanatical hatred of the Christian Dog which had somewhat abated for the two hundred years or so prior to the eleventh century. The Mohammedans became masters of Sicily in 878 and had appeared before Rome in 846. Their most northerly advance in France was stayed between Poitiers and Tours in 732 by Charles the Hammer, who flung them back beyond the Pyrenees; and at Vienna as late as 1529! The entire Mediterranean was a Moslem lake and its coasts are studded to-day with the remains of the towers where watch was kept for the dreaded lateen sail of the corsairs.

Therefore, when all of Western Europe except those portions under Mohammedan rule was whelmed in mental darkness, Christendom was almost surrounded by this virile, active civilization—for it was a real civilization of great refinement, learning, and cultivation; all the astronomical and astrological lore of the Semitic races, all the philosophy, practical and theoretical, of Aristotle, were theirs. During the passage of their faith from land to land the Moslems had evolved an architectural style, borrowed as concerned the main structural features from Persian or Sassanid buildings, which they spread through all the Mohammedan conquests. Saracenic and Moorish are thus two geographical designations of the arts practised by those who professed the Mohammedan faith. The dome and pointed horseshoe-shaped arches are distinguishing characteristic details. The long Moslem sojourns in Sicily and Spain affected strongly the Christian art of those countries. The seclusion of the women

Courtyard, or Cortile, of the CASA DE LAS CONCHAS in Salamanca, Spain. The architect is unknown. The design is illustrative of the freedom with which the Spanish artist worked. There are Gothic and Moorish influences mingled here with Renaissance forms.

MOHAMMEDAN LATTICED BAY WINDOWS, from which the women of the household could overlook street or courtyard, themselves unseen. The architects lavished much invention and ingenuity upon the woodwork of these overhanging lookouts, intricately pierced or filled with turned work.

An example of MOHAMMEDAN ARCHITECTURE, illustrating the use of colored tile and showing the horseshoe-shaped arches distinctive of Moorish and Saracenic work. Their faith forbidding the use of living forms, they fell back upon geometrical ornament and color.

THE COURTYARD OF A POMPEIIAN HOUSE, open to the sky, laid out in flowerbeds, adorned with sculpture and fountains. The walls behind the colonnade are decorated in vivid and beautiful color. Large houses had a number of such outdoor rooms.

and the jealous privacy of the family life of the Mohammedans expressed themselves in architecture by presenting to
the street a bare wall pierced by a door and an occasional
barred window and, high up, perhaps a heavily latticed projecting bay from which the women could catch a glimpse of
what was going on below without themselves being seen.
The houses were built around courtyards as has always been
the custom in warm climates and where women have been
denied freedom. The Greeks secluded their women also,
and while no remains of dwellings of an early date exist in
Greece itself, the Græco-Roman house, miraculously preserved to us by the eruption of Vesuvius which overwhelmed
Pompeii and Herculaneum, probably perpetuates the general disposition of rooms and courtyards customary in the
mother country. The Roman house and the Roman villa
followed Græco-Roman lines and we may still trace this old
tradition in the buildings of the Renaissance in Italy. But
in Spain the Moorish occupation lasted so long—the Moris-
cos, as they were called, were not driven from Granada by
Ferdinand and Isabella until 1492 and were not expelled
from Spain until 1609—that the Moorish character, its
distinctive distribution of walls and openings, is stamped
indelibly upon the architecture of Spain. To the Mohammedans we are indebted, in Sicily, in Southern Italy, and in
Spain, for glazed tile domes in color and the use of colored
faience in architectural decoration.

The rise and spread of Mohammedan faith, arms, civilization, arts, and sciences, is one of the most interesting as it is
one of the most eloquent exemplars of what has been said
in a previous chapter of the forces which unite to mould
the simplest bit of art. Unlike the arts of Egypt, Assyria,
and even of Greece and Rome, the steps of its progress being
comparatively modern are practically unbroken and readily

traced, and the action and reaction between them and the arts contemporaneous with them, easily observed and verified.

One bright spot gleams in Christian Europe in the Dark Ages when hope of an intellectual revival burns for a space during the reign of Charlemagne; but when he passed the arts sunk into a deeper lethargy.

Meanwhile, the Scandinavian tribes, restless explorers, had spread through Northern Europe and were gradually absorbed by the populations except a small colony in the northern part of France. These were the Normans or Northmen. They remained here quite tranquilly for a century or so, when, the old Norse spirit of wandering adventure reasserting itself, they sailed to Spain, to Sicily, and Italy, and succeeded in establishing footholds there. These expeditions and their great subsequent adventure, the conquest of England under William the Conqueror in 1066, were of much importance in the arts, for to them is due the dissemination of the style we know as Norman. A style of architecture, the Romanesque, had been slowly shaping itself in Italy and France, partially due to the presence of the remains of Roman buildings everywhere, a style exhibiting the unscientific features of all primitive building in piers and walls and arches far too heavy for the tasks they were called upon to perform. The Norman style is one of the forms of early Romanesque; and out of the Romanesque grew the Gothic, as we shall see.

Just prior to the year 1000 A. D. a superstition is said to have prevailed in Western Europe that the world would be destroyed in that year, and this fear paralyzed all progress of every sort. Many who wished to be on the safe side flocked to the monasteries and nunneries. When the eleventh century dawned and found the prediction unfulfilled a new impetus was given to industries of all kinds. The great monastic institutions naturally took the initiative—for to them had retired the larger proportion of the more intellectual classes, partly through fear of destruction at the close of the first millennium and the desire for spiritual preparation for the event, and partly because in them alone was to be found a peaceful refuge from the anarchy that prevailed in the outer world. The religious excitement created in all classes by the fear of the Judgment Day, augmented by a sense of relief that translation to a better land was deferred, was intensified by the reports of pilgrims fresh from Palestine where the Tomb of the Saviour was in the possession of the Infidel. In 1095 Europe rose, petty feuds were abandoned, and hundreds of thousands enrolled themselves as Soldiers of God, pledging themselves to the recovery of the Holy Places and the extermination of the Paynim. Once more Europe, by this and the subsequent Crusades, was brought into contact with the East; and, of far greater significance, the peoples of Europe were for the first time united in a common cause of common interest, on a lofty spiritual plane.

CHAPTER XV

THE MIDDLE AGES

The Monastic Orders — The Monastic or Romanesque Style — The Rise of
the Lay Spirit — The Gothic Style, the Architecture of the Communes —
French and English Gothic — The Spirit of Gothic not Congenial to the
Italians — Gothic in the Netherlands and Spain — Gothic Architecture
a System of Construction — The Great Cathedrals of France — The
Significance of Gothic.

ONE of the forces ready to be utilized in an awakening
world was the monastic orders, among them the Clunisian;
the powerful monastery of Cluny in France was independent
of either secular or episcopal power and acknowledged no authority save that of the Pope; Clunisian monks took numer-
ous journeys to all the countries of Europe and established
many branches of the order. At Cluny, as a consequence of
the constant intercourse kept up between this as a centre
and its offshoots in Italy and elsewhere, a strong school of
architects, sculptors, and painters was formed. Schools
were organized in which both the monks of the order and
the laity were instructed. The Cluniacs had established
their monasteries in many cases upon the ruins or in the
remains of old Roman buildings, and the architecture of these
had naturally the strongest influence upon the increasing
passion for building. Churches began to rise, exhibiting
new arrangements and modulations of the old forms of architecture, suited to the needs of the time. There is a remarkable
unity in the style of all the buildings erected everywhere
during this period, which only received such modifications
as materials at hand or some difference in local taste might
dictate. Thus, this style, the Romanesque or Monastic, is

rather inclined to refinement and delicacy in Southern
France, and in Normandy is bold and sturdy, expressive in
each case of the nature of the people. As remarked above,
for the first time Christian mankind was united in a common
bond of spiritual sympathy, for all the peoples of Europe
were enlisted under the banner of the Cross, and this contributed to the spread and unity of the new style. In the
south of France we find the influence of Byzantium in the
ornament. In the North, ornament is more abstract, less
related to or dependent upon vegetable forms, and we find
zigzag lines and various arbitrary treatments of the stone-
work to give light and shadow. In all districts grotesques
of animals and the human figure were used extensively.
Little by little the Abbey of Cluny became more and more
refined and luxurious and the work of the order began to
reflect this elegance; workmanship had arrived at a high
pitch of excellence; more and more daring experiments in
construction were tried and the time was ready for the
next stage.

The Clunisians were by no means the only monkish order.
There were the Cistercians, whose headquarters were in
Burgundy at Citeaux; the Benedictines, founded in Southern
Italy in the sixth century by Saint Benedict, who ordered
that all branches of art should be taught by the order; the
Augustinian, very like the Benedictine; the Carthusian
order, whose chief seat was the Grande Chartreuse near
Grenoble in France; the Dominican and Franciscan orders,
preaching friars; and many others. The whole period of art
from the seventh and eighth centuries to the twelfth has been
aptly called Monastic as well as Romanesque; the term very
accurately indicates its immediate human origin as Romanesque does its material, less direct, derivation.

The increase of luxury and license in some of the orders

had brought discredit upon all, as monastic life with all its negation of the inherent nobility, courage, and independence of the human soul was doing everywhere. And in spite of the fact that the Papal power and that of the bishops and princes of the Church had been steadily increasing and were to rise to their zenith in the thirteenth century, the laity began to feel their own strength and a sense of their dignity as men, to throw off monastic fetters and refuse to look at life through glasses colored by clerical thought. And the Lay or Gothic Spirit arose. And as its visible sign the style that reigned supreme in Europe during three centuries and influenced the work of two more, the Gothic or Mediæval, the architecture of the Communes, came into being.

The countries and nations of Western Europe, England, France, Spain, Italy, Germany, were beginning to define themselves.

Broadly speaking, the Gothic style developed in France in the twelfth century, reached its perfection in the thirteenth, and began to decline thereafter. We find at the close of the twelfth century a style transitional between Romanesque and Gothic in which both the round and the pointed arch occur; the Primary period in the thirteenth century; the Secondary in the fourteenth; and the Tertiary in the fifteenth, known as the Flamboyant from the flamelike lines of the window tracery. Between each of these periods in their full development are transitions shading off into each. In England, the period from the end of the twelfth to the end of the thirteenth centuries is designated as Early English and Advanced Early English; during the fourteenth, Early and Late Decorated; and, from the end of the fourteenth to the middle of the sixteenth when England began to feel the belated influence of the Renaissance, Early and Advanced Perpendicular and Tudor.

The CATHEDRAL OF LAON, France, a splendid specimen of very early Gothic. The oxen in the corner canopies of the towers are effigies of those which drew the stone for the edifice up the steep hill which rises suddenly out of a vast plain.

Interior of the CHURCH OF SAN MARCO in Venice, one of the most beautiful interiors in the world, dating from 1063 A.D., rich in colored marbles and bronze, and vaulted ceilings of gold mosaic mellowed by time into marvellous tones.

The Church of the ABBAYE-AUX-DAMES, at Caen, in Normandy, founded by Matilda, Queen of William the Conqueror, in 1062 A.D. to expiate the sin of marriage within the forbidden degree of relationship. A light and graceful example of Norman architecture.

NOTRE DAME DE PARIS, one of the noblest churches in Christendom. This, the principal, façade is designed with an orderly and majestic sobriety recalling Classic design at its best. A work of the thirteenth century, the finest period in Gothic art.

In the first period of French Gothic the ornament is rather naturalistic, in the second almost entirely so, and in the third it begins to stiffen into conventionalized types of, nevertheless, luxuriant growth. In every period figure sculpture is freely and finely employed in statues of saints, figures of animals, and grotesques. The ornamental forms are usually copied or conventionalized from the flora of the district in which each building is erected. In English Gothic the ornament varies with the period much more strongly; in Early English the foliage is so highly conventionalized that it is difficult to say from what it is derived; in the Decorated period it tends toward naturalism and we recognize the ivy, the grape, and oak; in the Perpendicular it becomes conventionalized again and all the architectural lines begin to stiffen as though they felt the impending changes of the Renaissance. It is curious to compare the third period of French Gothic, so full of fire and freedom, with the English third period, so rigid and restrained.

Gothic art never flourished in Italy as it did in the North; classical tradition was too strong to permit the new style more than a superficial modification of structure. It was never liked by the Italians, who failed to understand it as a fundamental constructive system and inclined strongly to adhere to their native, Roman, principles. In the Netherlands the style was affected by both French and German influences, and in Spain it is impure although interesting from the luxury of its forms, and has certain analogies with the Gothic of the Netherlands due no doubt to the conquest of the Low Countries by Spain.

Gothic architecture is above all a constructive system. The mere application of characteristic details of decorative carving or of window tracery to a structure does not proclaim it Gothic in principle. The fundamental principle of Gothic construction is that of counter-balancing a thrust by a thrust. Thrust is the force or push exerted by the weight of any mass upon some other mass. In an arch each of the wedge-shaped arch stones, voussoirs as they are called, presses against its fellow and transmits its own weight and part of whatever weight the arch as a whole is carrying. This pressure, push, thrust, is therefore carried down from stone to stone to the wall or pier which supports the arch. In Roman work these forces were absorbed in great masses of masonry, and the Monastic, Romanesque architecture followed in the same path until the master builders gradually learned to perforate these great thick walls with arches, and became so well acquainted, empirically at least, with the lines these thrusts follow, that they were able eventually in the full Gothic period to do away with walls altogether as a structural system, and to build merely a series of isolated piers to support the arches and the weights of vault and roof and the light screen-walls needed to enclose the building. Hence the splendid windows occupying the whole space from pier to pier of a Gothic cathedral and the added wonder of their glass. The thrust of an arch or vault was met by the thrust of another arch or vault so that one just neutralized the other; the architects became more and more daring, the vaults soared ever higher, the supports became ever more slender until at last, as at Beauvais, the limit was reached and the fabric collapsed.

This structural principle suddenly flowered in the Île de France, the district which included Paris, Rheims, Amiens, and Beauvais, and some of the adjacent provinces, into the most glorious structures the genius of man has ever raised. It was a spontaneous and natural outcome of the new-won freedom, of the mind from the monks, and of the body from the feudal oppressions of the noblesse; and it was the Com-

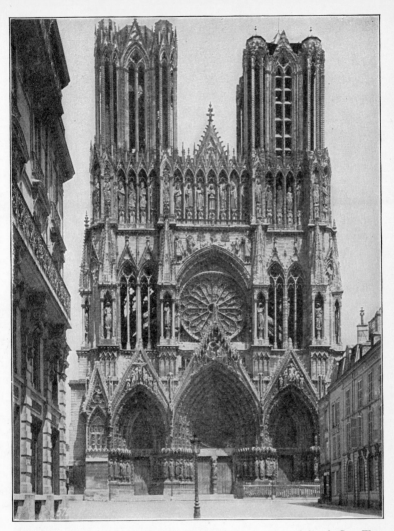

The CATHEDRAL OF NOTRE DAME, RHEIMS, France, as it was before the Great War. Begun about 1211 A. D. and mutilated and almost destroyed by the Germans, a crime that can never be expiated. One of the five greatest Mediæval cathedrals: Bourges, 1190; Chartres, 1194; Notre Dame de Paris, 1200; Rheims, 1211; and Amiens, 1220, built at the height of the Gothic period. The statuary, the stained glass, and the tapestries of Rheims were among the most precious possessions of mankind.

munes who gave their money, their hearts, and their brawn, to the erection of these great flowers in stone quivering upward to God. The period of burgeoning coincides with the growth of the French Kingdom, gradually consolidating the many counties and dukedoms of that time into the France we know. The Communes were friendly to the King, and worked upon their churches under the leadership of their bishops as though enlisted in a new Crusade. The glories of the cathedrals of Notre Dame de Paris, of Rheims, of Amiens, Laon, Chartres, and the Sainte Chapelle in Paris, in wrought stone, in sculpture, in stained and painted glass, in hangings of tapestry, in embroideries, goldsmiths' work, were like ecstatic prayers. And then, the first impulse exhausted, we find many of the northern communities lavishing their efforts and their treasure upon their secular buildings, a natural manifestation of the growing wealth and power of the burghers and of an awakening civic consciousness; and such structures as the Palais de Justice at Rouen arose, together with many private houses in stone, in brick and stone, and in half-timber.

Superficially no two styles would seem more dissimilar than the Gothic and the Greek; as systems of construction this is true; but in matters of detail they are based upon precisely the same principle, the basic principle of all plastic art: the use, control, and direction of the play of light. The profiles of Greek and Gothic mouldings are wonderfully similar and define the outlines of surfaces on which the play of direct and reflected light is modulated in precisely the same way, through a profound knowledge and thoughtful application of the same principle. Not until Bramante's work, at the very height of the Renaissance, do we encounter it again.

To some minds the Gothic period in art means the spiritual

aspirations of man expressed through buildings dedicated to the service of God, the impulse wholly religious. It may be suggested, however, that spiritually the Western World was under the rule of the Church, that is to say of the priesthood, and that while the laity labored with and for it, they frequently did so with reservations, if not with the tongue in the cheek—a state of mind indicated by the many ribald and scurrilous jokes upon the clergy and monks carved in wood and stone in the cathedrals and churches of the Middle Ages. Others look upon it as the early stage in the emancipation of the human reason from priestly control, as a visible sign of the mental as well as the spiritual unrest of the times, finding in these vast fabrics an outlet for unformulated aspirations toward the freedom of the soul, the dignity of man as man. There is a view suggested by Guizot that in the very earliest days of Christianity the Christian congregations were essentially democratic, electing their clergy and bishops; that this freedom they speedily lost and for centuries the invincible spirit of liberty in man, his passionate craving for self-government, his predisposition to think for himself, were in dumb and desperate conflict with a theocratic oligarchy, a despotic Church which demanded that her children should surrender to her and her clergy their very right to independent thought, and that after the eleventh century these aspirations toward personal liberty could no longer be suppressed. The student should read the whole history of the period and choose his own interpretation.

The buildings were rich with sculpture of great vitality and character, but of sculpture independent of architecture there was little save the mortuary portrait figures on the tombs of the great. Of painting there was little, of color there was a great deal—in other words, of the art of representation, aside from very conventional figures of Divine

LA SAINTE CHAPELLE, erected for Louis the Good, designed by Pierre de Montereau, 1245 A. D., to contain the sacred relics brought back from the Holy Land in 1239. The interior was restored in polychrome under the direction of Viollet-le-Duc.

The Interior of WESTMINSTER ABBEY, the Pantheon of Great Britain, in which may be traced the principal periods of English Gothic architecture, Early English, Decorated, and Early and Late Perpendicular. Begun in London about 1220 A. D.

The Interior of AMIENS CATHEDRAL. The nave is 140 feet high to the stone vaulting, and the roof is 60 feet higher. Every moulding of the vaulting ribs has its own supporting colonnette soaring to the spring of the vault.

The CATHEDRAL OF AMIENS, begun 1220 A. D. and completed about 1288. It is considered to be, in plan and interior design, the fine flower of the Gothic style in France. The towers are of the fourteenth and early fifteenth centuries.

Personages, there was little, but of the decorative coloration of statues and of the walls, piers, and vaults of buildings there was much, and all the new-found glory of stained and painted glass. The textile arts had flourished all through the Dark Ages, for people must be clothed; and in this art, in that of enamelling, and in rude works in gold and silver, as well as in mosaics of glass and colored marbles of Byzantine workmanship, we are able to trace more clearly even than in architecture the reactions of people upon people, of art upon art.

CHAPTER XVI

THE DAWN OF THE RENAISSANCE

The Middle Age the Chrysalis of the Renaissance — Benvenuto Cellini and His Religious Faith — The Corruption of the Church — Political Conditions Precedent to the Renaissance — Guelph and Ghibelline — The Rise of the Italian Communes or Republics — They Fall into the Hands of Despots — The Italian Tongue — Dante — Cimabue — Giotto — Pisano — Brunelleschi a Link Between the Art of the Old Era and of the New — The Invention of Printing — The Fall of Constantinople — The Passion for Learning — The Rebirth of the Mind and Soul of Man, the Renaissance.

THE monkish robe of the Middle Age is like that rough brown pupa which hides in its heart the folded wings of the butterfly; for the Middle Age is the chrysalis of the Renaissance and the origins of that great unfolding of the spirit of men lie deep within it. The Renaissance is but the flowering, on soil congenial to it and under circumstances of felicitous concurrence, of seed long sown. In France and in Italy, in the poetry of Provence and the poetry of Dante, in the spirit of the Communes of both countries, that Lay Spirit which reared the cathedrals of the Middle Age, we find it shadowed forth. It is merely the continuance of the long process of restoration to man of his rightful intellectual inheritance, temporarily abated by the blight that followed the hoof of the Hun.

Who shall be bold enough to say of the mind or soul of man that one impulse is purely religious, another purely intellectual, deny everything but a blind and somewhat stupid religiosity to the man of the Middle Age and deny everything but a cold and cynical intellectuality to the men of the Renaissance? That is not the way men are made.

PORTAL FIGURES from the Cathedral of
CHARTRES, early French Gothic sculpture of a truly architectonic type; the human
figure is elongated and decoratively treated so
as to contribute harmoniously to the architectural effect of the whole great portal.

The Cathedral of NOTRE DAME DE
CHARTRES, on the River Eure, dedicated
in 1260 A. D., is one of the most beautiful in
France. Its stained glass is glorious and is
only rivalled by that of Rheims and La Sainte
Chapelle.

COURTYARD OF THE BARGELLO, in Florence, begun in 1255 A. D. and for 300 years
the residence of the Podestà, or chief magistrate, of Florence; later a prison and office of the Bargello
or chief of police. Now used as a museum of priceless masterpieces of Italian art. The staircase was built about 1345 and the walls of the court are covered with the coats of arms of successive
Podestàs. A beautiful example of the Italian Gothic style.

They are compact of many interwoven strands of thought and feeling. Read the autobiography of Benvenuto Cellini, that fiery braggart and murderer, exquisite artificer in gold and enamels; read of his passion for work, his worship of beauty, his devout and naïf religion. He draws his own portrait with the utmost simplicity, in black and white with no intermediate gradations, and we see, incarnate in him, the conflicting promptings of the spirit of his day in a light that illumines the whole period for us. In the Middle Age man found God and when he had found him, secure and serene in his faith, applied his energies to the recovery of the germs of political freedom, liberty of thought and of conscience, and his lost intellectual birthright. The history of man is but the story of his long struggle upward through the ages toward Liberty. The Church had strayed far from the simple teaching of the Carpenter of Nazareth, abuses had grown up within it, and the Throne of Grace was obscured by a vast company of intercessionary saints. In the many prayers Cellini offers up in the course of his life it is observable that he addresses them directly to the Deity and never calls upon any saint to act as intermediary. This seems indicative of a generally prevalent state of mind—of which there are many confirmations—in which a plentiful cynicism is felt toward the Church and its inventions but in which the Christian faith remains unshaken. The Church was one of the dominant factors in personal and political life, and had become worldly, unspiritual, devoured by mundane political ambitions, corrupt and unscrupulous; and the Renaissance cannot be clearly understood unless these facts are recognized with all their consequences and implications.

As Greece had been a group of little city-states, constantly at odds with each other and changing sides as their temporary advantage pointed, so was Italy in the Middle Age. The

Papacy was endeavoring to add supremacy in the political world to her domination in the spiritual. The shadow of the Roman Empire, with a shadowy Emperor of German birth at its apex, lay upon the Western world. The Pope claimed that as the Vicar of Christ and therefore the superior of all other earthly sovereigns, he must crown the Emperor; the Emperor demurred; both potentates were constantly seeking to encroach upon the rights and authority, real or assumed, of the other, and the bitter feud between them and their adherents, the Guelph and Ghibelline parties, entangled all Italy and much of Europe in the meshes of a thousand political intrigues, plots, and counterplots. This miserable struggle exhausted all factions including the burgher class, which had gradually learned to reap the advantage of all these quarrels, as the Communes of France had done, and had acquired the real balance of power; and the little republics of Italy sought refuge from conflict and its responsibilities under the banners of the Despots.

By the twelfth century the Germanic tongue of the descendants of the Barbarians, and of the Longobards who had been settled for hundreds of years in that wide plain of Lombardy to which they had given their name, was completely absorbed, and the Italian language, enriched by these foreign additions was, in spite of local dialectic differences that persist to this day in every village and province, a flexible, sonorous, and melodious vehicle of thought and feeling of a definitely Latin cast. Dante Alighieri, with whom not only culminates the Middle Age in Italy, but is inaugurated the new era, cast aside the Latin language of the scholar and wrote the *Divine Comedy* in the vulgar tongue with a mediæval heart and a modern mind. For the first time a work of literature was accessible to the common people, who pointed out Dante on the streets as the man who

*A portion of THE TRIBUTE MONEY, a fresco painted by MASACCIO in the Bran-
cacci Chapel of the Church of the Carmine in Florence. A triptych (a picture in three panels
side by side) without the usual separation between them. Masaccio was called "the deliverer
of painting" when Florentine painting was in danger of falling into rote and formula.
Michael Angelo and Raphael recognized the genius of this young painter, who was born in
or near Florence in 1401 and disappeared in 1427 when he was on his way to Rome.*

*The DEATH OF ST. FRANCIS OF ASSISI, by GIOTTO (Angiolotto Bondoni) in the
Church of Santa Croce, the Westminster Abbey of Florence. One of a series depicting the
life of St. Francis, done at the height of Giotto's powers. Born in 1266 and dying in 1337, the
friend of the immortal Dante, pupil of Cimabue, the contemporary of Boccaccio, he marks the
transition from the hierarchical style of the Byzantine school and is one of the great precursors
of the Renaissance.*

had descended into Hell. In painting, the rising sap of modern thought was first manifested in Dante's friend Cimabue, who made a departure from the stiff and lifeless convention of the Byzantine tradition and drew the figure from life instead of repeating an established flat pattern as the custom had been; his picture of the Madonna was greeted as a miracle by the people of Florence and escorted by joyous crowds in a shower of flower petals to its place in the Church of Santa Maria Novella. His pupil Giotto, painter, sculptor, and architect, a broader man and a better artist, abandoned to a great extent the use of gold backgrounds, went to life for his inspiration, and introduced the element of landscape into his compositions. In sculpture, Niccola Pisano, through the study of antique Roman fragments of carving, opened a vista which led to the exquisite works of a galaxy of artists. And in architecture our first debt is to Filippo Brunelleschi for his examination of Roman buildings and the application of their constructive and decorative principles to his own work. Brunelleschi is a true link in architecture between the Middle Age and the Renaissance as Dante is in literature, although he came much later, for architecture responded last to the new impulse; in his lifetime printing was invented and the art of paper-making was introduced from China to work a revolution in the intellectual world by the rapid and cheap distribution of the classics of ancient literature. Seven years after his death in 1446 the Turks took Constantinople, and swarms of scholars and artists took refuge in Italy, bearing with them copies of many of the classic authors, Roman and Greek. A mad enthusiasm for this new-found culture of the ancients seized the strong intellects refreshed as it were by the long sleep of the Dark and Middle Ages. The monasteries of Europe were ransacked for classical manuscripts which had been kept from the world for ages by the ignorance, stupidity, or bigotry of the monks, or preserved by the loving care of the instructed. Scholars lectured everywhere and the universities overflowed with students from every corner of Europe who flocked starving to this feast of knowledge spread for all who would partake. The myths of Greece and Rome became familiar and soon the immortal stories of the pagan gods began to be portrayed in art often in strange association with Christian legend.

At a time when English noblemen and the French noblesse scorned the ability to read and write as being beneath the dignity of the man of blood and action, the aristocracy of Italy were eagerly absorbing all this learning; to their fresh and virile minds was given the knowledge of the past in the literature of humanism, and they entered into their restored heritage of mental freedom. As in the Athens of the Golden Age, the ground prepared, the seed sown, a harvest of vivid and versatile personalities far exceeding in number the contemporaries of Pericles sprang up to make the period glorious. Like that other Golden Age the period was brief—from about 1400 in the youth of Brunelleschi to the death in 1564 of Michael Angelo, who had long mourned its decline. And the flood of this mental and spiritual rebirth bore on its bosom such argosies of beauty as only Athens ever sheltered or sent forth.

The stream of antique learning that poured into Italian minds so swiftly, filling them in so short a time with strange new beauties and stranger flowers of evil, swept away in its sudden and powerful rush many of the old spiritual props of an earlier and simpler age. Precious as the knowledge of good and evil is, man paid for it, as he has ever paid, a heavy price; but who would not rather pay that price than dwell in darkness, half-souls, half-minds, half-men! Dazzled at first by the light that beat upon their eyes. it seemed as

The *MEETING OF S. FRANCIS AND S. DOMINIC, a lunette or semi-circular panel over a doorway in the Loggia di S. Paolo in Florence, in glazed and colored terra-cotta, executed by LUCA DELLA ROBBIA, born 1400, died 1482. Luca, who as a sculptor ranks close to Donatello, chose to work in clay and color rather than in stone or bronze, although he worked in marble also. His brother and nephews continued the family tradition but in a somewhat inferior vein.*

The PALAZZO COMMUNALE of Piacenza, an excellent specimen of the Mediæval Town Hall in Northern Italy, usually containing an immense meeting-hall in the principal story, and often a market-place under the open arcades at the street level. Built about 1281.

The Church of S. MARIA DELLE GRAZIE in Milan, by BRAMANTE, the greatest architect of the Italian Renaissance, erected in brick and terra-cotta between 1492 and 1497. Here the Gothic tradition of Lombardy was reconciled with the Classic revival.

though there must be two kinds of truth, the pagan and the
Christian truth. But presently men like Pico della Mirandola, that keen intellect and fine spirit, endeavored to rec-
oncile the newly acquired learning with the tenets of the
Christian faith, dimly perceiving that all truth is one, that
the instinct of man is to erect beyond the confines of his
own soul an ideal of goodness and beauty immerging all the
virtues he would fain himself possess.

Throughout the Renaissance in Italy vice stalked abroad
at virtue's side, even in the very garments of virtue. With
the simplicity and gravity of manners of the early Florentine
republic is to be contrasted the wickedness of the Papal
Court of the Borgias. Poison and piety, the poniard and
the psaltery, the dungeon and the sunlit reaches of fair
gardens, were contrasts that did not exclude a true and
passionate love of the arts of design, of literature, of music,
of poetry, a noble thirst for knowledge careless of its good
or evil import be it but knowledge. The depravity of a Cesare Borgia, incestuous fratricide, is balanced by the virtues
of a Girolamo Savonarola, priest and patriot, who held the
hearts of Florence in his hands. Happy the ruler who, secure
in the affections of his people and of his family, could dispense
with the shirt of mail that for his fellow princes, worn se-
cretly beneath their dress, on so many occasions blunted the
dagger of the assassin. In the palaces of Venice, of Naples,
of most Italian cities, the *bravi* who would cut you a throat
like winking were accepted appurtenances of a noble house.
A tolerance of these contrasts and the facts they represented,
the acceptance of them as normal conditions, strange and
amazing to present-day thought, pervaded Italian society.
The versatility of the epoch, that showed itself in the artist
who was goldsmith, painter, architect, engineer, sculptor,
scientist, designer of pageants, poet, companion of savants

and princes, was frequently manifested in the prince by the combination in him of the extreme of urbanity and amenity with a simple ruthlessness that takes one's twentieth-century breath away.

Little by little the Italians became the bankers of Europe; the quays of Venice and Genoa, as those of Pisa and Amalfi had been in earlier times, were piled high with the carpets and tissues, the gold and jewels and ivory of the East; and with the wealth of the world that poured into the lap of Italy came the luxuries of a spacious life, luxuries that have always seemed in the history of the world to sap the foundations of civil life and bring decay of moral fibre, of civic virtue, in their train, leaving the people the prey of others whom soft living has not yet enfeebled. Two hundred years sufficed for Italy to pass through every phase from the utmost simplicity of manners to utter decadence. Men lived fast in those days and quickly exhausted every attainable sensation, exhausted themselves, their stock, and their nation.

In their fearless curiosity the men of the Renaissance explored every avenue of thought and feeling, made every political experiment—democracy in Florence, theocracy in Rome, aristocratic oligarchy in Venice, monarchy in Naples, tyranny in Milan; this diversity in their political institutions is but one sign of their mental activity and unrest, as Symonds points out. Variety and individuality are revealed in their arts as we should expect; and these are exemplified in a large way by the physiognomy of their cities, an individuality fostered by those conditions of climate, of situation, of wide horizons like Venice or of mountainous isolation like Siena or San Gimignano, with many other of the factors we indicated in an earlier chapter as contributing to the moulding of character, human or artistic. All these influences wrought upon the Italian artist, completely the child of his

The *PALAZZO STROZZI. in Florence,* ascribed to *BENEDETTO DA MAIANO* and finished by Cronaca. Commenced for Filippo Strozzi, the corner-stone was laid to the music of flutes one spring day in 1489. A typical Florentine palace, dignified, severe, and strong.

The *CAPELLA PAZZI, in Florence, by BRUNELLESCHI, embellished with the sculpture of Donatello and of the Della Robbias.* Possessing the freedom of the Mediæval period with the charm of the Early Renaissance, inaugurated by this remarkable group of Florentine masters.

The *DOME OF THE CATHEDRAL OF FLORENCE and the CAMPANILE.* The Dome was built between 1420 and 1434 by *FILIPPO BRUNELLESCHI,* a Florentine sculptor turned architect, born about 1377, died about 1446. He and his friend Donatello were the actual inaugurators of the Renaissance in architecture and sculpture in Italy. The Campanile, by *GIOTTO,* adorned with sculpture by some of the best masters of Florence, was begun about 1395, when he was employed upon the Cathedral, and completed in 1387, after his death.

hour. After many centuries we are again able to identify the man with his work as we may in Greece. In Italy from Cimabue on, we know every artist of any significance whatever, the circumstances of his life and the number and quality of his works. The biographies and critical analyses and monographs on the Renaissance period are legion; and we must resist a temptation to develop the many fascinating and interlocking themes beyond the limits proper to so swift a summary as we are making here. The Renaissance is the time of personality, sharp cut, yet full of apparent contradictions which yield only to a long and thoughtful study of the period. These men must be apprehended as essentially simple, with a direct and simple outlook on their world. Their reactions to the stimuli of the moment are as many and diverse as the stimuli themselves, as diversified as the spirit of the time, and the reactions being direct and simple their sum produces the impression of a complexity of character they did not really possess. A modern man is a much more complex person. It was as though they kept their morality, their religion, their politics, their culture, in separate compartments of the brain so that they could not interact, and, for a modern mind in which all sorts of inhibitions and interactions are in conflict and make every action an affair of questioning and self-searching, it is difficult to find and maintain a sympathetic and understanding attitude—doubly difficult for a Protestant mind, against whose spiritual background the flames of hell-fire leap and flicker. The man of the Renaissance was relieved of all Protestant prohibitions and inhibitions and moved straight to his goal whatever that might be, through blood or tears.

It was in this atmosphere created by simple but conflicting elements that the artist of the Renaissance lived and worked. And the strange and naïf commingling of simple

Christian belief and piety with simple pagan behavior is his reaction to their stimuli. Simple as the Renaissance mind was compared with the modern mind, it was complex compared with the simplicity of Greek or Roman. The Christian religion had changed for good and all the outlook of Western civilization upon life and a whole new order of ideas, thoughts, emotions, had arisen for which the sculpture of Greece, the architecture of Rome or of the Communes were inadequate, and could only find a measure of expression in the art of painting, to rise in this epoch to heights undreamed.

CHAPTER XVII

THE RENAISSANCE IN ITALY

DAWN, mid-day and dusk; infancy, maturity, and old age; seed, fruit, and decay; eternal triads, the fate of all created things; a sequence eternally renewed so that decline is but the step that precedes the birth of something new; not to be regarded with repining and regret, but to be accepted as the natural order in the world; the art of the Renaissance passed through these three inevitable stages of transition from one state of being to another, as Grecian and Gothic had passed. To see the beauty in each, to learn the lesson each offers to our view, not to wish that this work were more mature, this not quite so over-ripe; not to expect the qualities of a Michael Angelo in a Botticelli—wishes vain and unfruitful; this is the business of the artist and the student of art alike.

What has been already said upon the general characteristic complexity of the period in Italy must suffice as an atmospheric envelope, through which we may occasionally throw a cross light illuminating some salience of personality or manners. The names that crowd in upon us, each evoking a swarm of associations and ideas, are countless; their mention without developing these mental pictures would be a mere stupid list; our frame is too small to contain many and we must therefore concentrate our attention upon a few, to typify in each stage of the art of Italy in the Renaissance the major traits of that stage or of that personality.

We have mentioned Cimabue, Giotto, and Pisano as being precursors of the Renaissance in the Middle Age itself. These men and the group that immediately followed them laid the foundations upon which the structure of Italian Renaissance art arose. Painting and sculpture were developing a technique and a point of view; architecture lingered behind her younger sisters in Mediæval by-ways, and it was not until she was led across the borders of the fifteenth century by Brunelleschi that she forsook them for the Roman road where Italian genius moved with freedom.

In 1402 this Filippo Brunelleschi, a young sculptor, disappointed in not receiving the award in the competition won by Lorenzo Ghiberti for the bronze doors of the Baptistery of Florence—later declared by Michael Angelo worthy of being the gates of Paradise—foreswore sculpture and took the road for Rome with his young friend Donatello to study architecture. These two boys, Donatello but sixteen and Brunelleschi nine years his senior, threw themselves with the ardor of their age and the precocity of their time into the study of classical antiquity in Rome, pursuing their researches far out into the Campagna. After five years Filippo returned to Florence to secure the commission to erect a dome over the crossing of nave and transepts of Arnolfo's Cathedral of Santa Maria del' Fiore. After some time he persuaded the Syndics of his ability, was given the work and carried it to its superb conclusion despite many vicissitudes and hindrances, including the unwelcome association with him of his old rival Ghiberti. He adorned his native city with

THE LIBRARY, CAMPANILE, SAN MARCO, and THE PALACE OF THE DOGES from the Canale di San Marco. The Library, by SANSOVINO, is entirely of creamy white Istrian marble weathered black in places; the Palace, of Verona and Istrian marbles, rose and cream. The Campanile is of pale red brick, the upper part of Istrian, the roof grey-green copper. San Marco is of every soft and beautiful hue that old marble and mosaic assume with the passage of time.

The CA' D'ORO, or Golden House, so called because much of the carved decoration was originally gilded. It was built upon the Grand Canal in Venice about 1421 for Piero Contarino by MATTEO RAVERTI, GIOVANNI BUON, and BARTOLOMMEO BUON THE ELDER. The use of colored marbles, the cresting along the cornice, and the screens of pierced tracery thrown across a mass of shadow as in these loggias, are characteristic of this Gothic, so warm and sympathetic, so peculiarly Venetian.

many beautiful structures, works of real originality and genius, inspired by the principles of classic architecture but adapted to their modern uses. The Capella Pazzi, the Ospedale degli Innocenti, both embellished by the exquisite sculpture of Donatello and Della Robbia, and the stupendous Palazzo Pitti, are his; and he built fortifications at Pisa, and dams at Mantua to control the waters of the Po.

It is to be especially remarked of the work of the architects of the Early Renaissance that it is singularly free from mere imitation of antique motifs; it is truly creative; and it was reserved for the so-called High Renaissance, when the creative faculty in Italian art was exhausted, to imitate the Classic as closely as the men of the decadence were able, or feebly to attempt to follow the great gesture of Angelo.

Brunelleschi's friend and partner Donatello was by all accounts one of the simplest and most lovable artists of the Renaissance. Some of his work exhibits that touch of austerity, almost of awkwardness, to be seen in Phidian sculpture which, it will be recalled, was not only the transition from the primitive art of the pre-Periclean age but was in itself the culmination of all the great qualities of Greek sculpture; and, although it cannot be said of Donatello that in him culminates the sculpture of the Renaissance, he is the authentic link between the old order and the new and rises to heights unattained save by Michael Angelo himself. A man of versatility too, capable of the Saint George of Or San Michele in Florence, the superb equestrian statue of Gattamelata in Padua, and things of such wonderful spirituality, grace, beauty, and charm as the Saint Cecilia, the medallions of cherubs in the frieze of the Capella Pazzi, or the dancing children in the outdoor pulpit of the Duomo of Prato and for the organ loft of the Duomo of Florence. His was a truly sculptural gift, moving with power and sweetness within the limits of the craft and never straying into the barren fields of the merely pictorial where so many sculptors have lost themselves.

Of the painters contemporary with these simple giants of this early period we cannot but choose Masaccio, Ugly Tom, as he was affectionately called, a giant in stature as well as ability, a genius who started for Rome at twenty-seven and was never heard of again, vanishing without a trace from the perilous brigand-haunted highroads of Italy. Here was a remarkable man, far ahead of his time, to whose work the succeeding generation went to school. Raphael himself laid it under tribute and borrowed motifs from it. Through him the art of painting moves from infancy to maturity in one superb step with unhesitating authority. Atmosphere, movement, real light and air, a large sense of composition, breadth and dignity of treatment, modernity, suddenly appear in Italian painting. In his untimely and mysterious death the art of the world mourns the loss of a figure that gave promise of being ranged with the very greatest masters of painting of a later day.

It is always a matter for wonderment that men like Masaccio and Donatello and Raphael and a hundred others, should have produced such remarkable things in their youth. The time fostered precocious genius, it is true, but the training of the artist had much to do with it. Masaccio died at twenty-seven, Raphael at thirty-seven, with an immense amount of work of the highest quality behind them. But they, like their compeers, had begun their apprenticeship at a very early age, frequently at eight or nine or ten, learning the technical secrets of their trade—for trade it was— grinding colors, preparing panels, learning to draw and paint and model and carve; in very many cases the boy was apprenticed to a goldsmith, whose trade included all of the

Alto Relievo of the MADONNA AND CHILD, by MINO DA FIESOLE born at Fiesole, near Florence, 1431, and died 1484. One of the decorations of his Tomb of Hugo, Margrave of Tuscany, in the Church of the Badia, Florence.

A DECORATIVE MEDALLION by the DELLA ROBBIA family, in glazed polychrome terra-cotta, indicating the character of their work in this kind. In relief, in color, in the decorative use of leaves and living things, it is a model of perfection.

The S. CECILIA of DONATELLO, one of the most exquisite bas-reliefs in existence. This work, his superb and masculine Gattamelata, and his famous Singing Boys, indicate somewhat the range of this extraordinary and lovable genius, born in 1386, died 1466.

STATUE OF GATTAMELATA (Erasmo di Narni) by DONATELLO, ranking second only to that of Colleoni. The original, in bronze, is in Padua, and was cast in 1447, the first equestrian monument cast in Italy since Roman times.

arts of design, and he learned to set gems, work in the precious metals, cast bronze and chase it. So that by the age at which a boy in America is about to enter college, the boy of the Renaissance was a fully trained, perfectly equipped master of a number of delicate and difficult crafts. Architects passed through this same training; it gave a boy a thorough technical training in art in all its branches and his special bent declared itself later. Would that we might return to this principle in the education of the artist, encourage versatility and well-rounded training and combat the dangerous tendency toward a narrow specialism! For the architect the system had the defects of its merits; the emphasis upon the decorative, pictorial aspects of art and the apparent neglect in most instances to foster a sound knowledge of construction resulted in a fertility of invention in details and a weakness on the structural side that vitiates the worth of a great deal of the architecture of the Renaissance in Italy, so much of it charmingly irrational, delightfully untrue. But it was not a scientific age; the science of Renaissance architecture was to be developed much later, by the French.

Bramante Lazzari, the architect who planned Saint Peter's in Rome, Andrea Verocchio, sculptor and painter, teacher of Lionardo da Vinci, and Andrea Mantegna, the painter so long attached to the Gonzaga family in Mantua, may be selected as representative of the second stage, the period of full development, in which a robust and yet delicate sophistication effaces the marks of transition visible in the term just traversed. These men may be regarded, with Lionardo da Vinci who was only seventeen years younger than his master Verocchio, and with the two great figures of Michael Angelo and Raphael, as marking the highest level of Renaissance art, although in point of time Lionardo and Bramante were contemporaries and Angelo and Raphael were born twenty-five and thirty-five years later. Titian, the Venetian master, was, too, a contemporary of Michael Angelo; but it is usual to treat the Venetian school as lying outside the main current of Italian art just as Venice herself, politically and geographically, occupied a unique position. The intensely personal genius of Angelo accords him a place apart. Raphael is much more easily apprehended as the child of his time, of his training, and of the traditions in which he was nurtured. In his harmonious nature, in his highly sensitive artistic gifts, the æsthetics of art and its science, the golden clews that other men had followed were gathered up and woven into a splendid tissue of supreme accomplishment. So Raphael, while by no means the hero of the Renaissance, also has his place apart like Angelo, and like Lionardo, whose personality is one of the most fascinating of all time.

Bramante was born in Urbino. His first master was Mantegna, but his bent was architectural, and chance and a wandering foot led him through the cities of Lombardy and finally to Milan, where he emerges from obscurity about 1492 as the author of the lovely Santa Maria delle Grazie. He was then forty-eight. Three years later he began the beautiful Cancellaria in Rome, the offices of the Chancellor of the Roman Church. He must have returned to Milan, for he is supposed to have fled from there with Lionardo da Vinci when their patron Ludovico Sforza fell into the hands of Louis XII of France in 1499. He made as thorough a study as Brunelleschi of Roman and Græco Roman remains; these studies, and especially of those works transmitting Grecian inspiration, combined with the probable influence of the subtle Lionardo, and possible acquaintance with the refinements of the best Gothic architecture, must have turned his mind toward those subtleties and refine-

PORTRAIT OF ELISABETTA GON-ZAGA, Duchess of Urbino, by ANDREA MANTEGNA, born at Vicenza 1431, and died at Mantua in 1506. Court Painter to the Gonzaghe, Marquises and, later, Dukes of Mantua.

By JAN VAN EYCK, born in Flanders about 1386, the pupil of his elder brother, HUBERT, born 1366, died 1426. The invention of oil painting is sometimes ascribed to them. The brothers were strongly influenced by the early Venetians.

THE NATIVITY, a wood-engraving by ALBRECHT DÜRER, perhaps the greatest engraver on wood and copper who ever lived. He was born at Nuremberg, Germany, in 1471, and died there in 1548.

Portrait of BEATRICE D'ESTE by LIONARDO DA VINCI, born near Florence in 1452 and died in 1519. In color, in character, in draftsmanship, one of the most exquisite works of this master.

ments of which his work is full. The profile of every moulding is studied with the most sensitive care and the most
subtle science; his arcades are rhythmically spaced, the
openings toward the centre being of greater span; and the
curvature of horizontal lines seems to be the only Greek
refinement that was sealed from him.

He was, after executing such works as this Cancellaria
and the Court of the Belvedere in the Vatican, made Clerk
to the Signet in the Papal organization, and under Julius II
made his design for a new Saint Peter's to take the place of
the old basilica found to be too small to receive the huge
tomb which Julius projected for himself and which Michael
Angelo was to execute for him. The faults of Saint Peter's
as it exists to-day are not to be ascribed to Bramante nor to
his conception, but to the departures from that conception.
When, years later, Angelo was placed in charge of the work
he declared that all the changes proposed or made by other
architects since Bramante's death in 1514 were errors and
himself adhered as closely as circumstances permitted to
the original plan.

Bramante's position and appointments permitted him to
live in a very splendid manner. He brought his young nephew
Raphael to Rome and launched him in the Roman world.
When he died he was buried in the great church that crowned
his career, with every mark of honor that Rome could be-
stow upon his memory.

At ten years of age the name of Andrea Mantegna was
entered on the books of the guild of painters of Padua. All
his life he loved and studied the sculpture of Greece and
Rome, especially the bas-reliefs, and the reflection of this
interest informs all his dignified and distinguished painting.
At the age of twenty-seven he entered the household of
Ludovico Gonzaga, Marquis of Mantua, as painter-in-

ordinary and served three successive princes of that house except for a brief interlude when his services were loaned to Innocent VIII for the decoration of a chapel. His familiarity with classical lore, his collection of antiquities, a wide correspondence and intercourse with scholars, so imbued him with the spirit of the antique that in him Rome might have been said to live again. Cold as the marbles of his original inspiration at first, he learned to invest his majestic and suave compositions with an envelope of color adequate to his themes. He represents in a peculiar degree the type of artist who was able to satisfy the ardent desire of the time for some visualization of the glories of Italy's classical past. He was the acclaimed figure of his day in painting, although to modern taste the archæological flavor of his work, its constructed episodes and display of the erudition of the age, rob it of a living interest.

In her life of Isabella d' Este the Marchioness of Francesco Gonzaga, one of the three patrons of Mantegna, Miss Cartwright quotes a letter containing the most minute instructions for the concoction of a picture Isabella wished Perugino to execute, to occupy a place beside one of Mantegna's, the literary content, the symbolic and mythological allusions and significances, having been worked up for her by Paride da Ceresara, a humanist of her court. To clog the wings of a painter's spirit with such stuff is almost incredible; it marks a tendency that was to extinguish the spark of artistic inspiration in Italy.

Upon the one hand of Andrea Verocchio—Andrew Trueeye—is the influence of his master Donatello; on the other his own great pupil Lionardo continues a tradition of consummate craftsmanship. His best work, completed by the Venetian Leopardi, is the equestrian statue of the Bergamese captain of the forces of Venice, Bartolommeo Colleoni,

ALTARPIECE for the Church of the Frari in Venice, by GIOVANNI BELLINI, born about 1428 and died in 1516. He was a pupil of Gentile da Fabriano and came of a family of painters. He was of the second period of Venetian painting, a link between the Primitives and the last and greatest group—Titian, Tintoretto, Veronese, and Giorgione. This picture was painted in 1488; it is mellow, beautiful, and quiet, with a background simulating golden mosaic.

AN ALLEGORY OF SPRING by SANDRO BOTTICELLI, whose family name was Filipepi, born at Florence 1447, died in 1510; a painter of poetic visions in the dawn of the modern world. Lorenzo the Magnificent was his patron and he was a friend of Michael Angelo, then in his youth. This is a work of the Primitive School of Italian painting, and it was in paintings such as this that the Pre-Raphaelite group in England found their inspiration for design if not for color.

superb in workmanship, in sculptural quality appropriate to bronze, in portraiture and characterization, the supreme equestrian figure of the world. Verocchio's other principal works are in Florence, the city of his birth, among them the well-known David, the Doubting Thomas of Or San Michele, and the charming Boy with a Dolphin surmounting the fountain in the courtyard of the Palazzo Vecchio. Besides Lionardo da Vinci and Lorenzo di Credi the Florentines, Perugino the Umbrian was a pupil, and Perugino was the master of Raphael. So that two artists as divergent in temperament, point of view, and accomplishment, as Raphael and Lionardo derive from Donatello through Verocchio.

Compared with the tremendous output of the *bottega* of Raphael with his band of pupils and assistants, designing and executing mural paintings of imposing dimensions; decorating the Stanze and Loggia of the Vatican for the Pope; the Farnesina Palace with Baldassare Peruzzi for the Sienese banker Chigi; making cartoons for tapestries; designing architecture like the Palazzo Pandolfini in Florence; painting masterly portraits of Pope and great lady; compared with these overwhelming accomplishments of a life that was cut short at thirty-seven, the known works of Lionardo seem few indeed, and yet their beauty and their profound psychology cause them to rank among the most highly prized paintings in the world. It has been said of Lionardo that he was haunted by the ghost of a smile, the smile that lies behind the eyes of Mona Lisa and seems just about to move the quiet lips; the smile, faint and bewitching, that transpires through the countenance of La Belle Ferronière like a little candle faintly shining; the smile that seems to lie in the very texture of the skin and lurk in the shadows of his faun-like Saint John the Baptist. Of his Last

Supper nothing remains except the composition to speak of his mastery of that most difficult element of art, a mastery unquestionable. The color departed long since and the restorations give no idea of its original beauty, but even in its ruined and defaced condition the most immature observer must feel it to be a great picture.

In him is incarnated the versatility of the Renaissance and its artists. Of illegitimate birth, he possessed great personal dignity, magnetism, and beauty. The interest of Ludovico Sforza, so long his patron in Milan, was first aroused by his abilities as a musician, poet, and singer. But he was also an engineer of ingenuity, ability, and imagination, a natural philosopher who carried his researches into many fields in physics and natural history. He was a consummate draftsman and left a vast number of drawings executed with the most delicate care and showing how profoundly he studied tree, insect, plant, flower, man and woman, youth and old age, the beautiful and the grotesque. His life was serene; born near Florence in 1452 he was thus the contemporary of Bramante and his friend, twenty-three years older than Michael Angelo and thirty-one the senior of Raphael; but genius is not to be placed by the calendar, and these three, with Titian who was Leonardo's junior by twenty-five years and whose exceptionally long and prolific life carried the splendid tradition of an earlier time almost to the decadent close of the sixteenth century, rank apart together as the greatest artists of this marvellously fecund period and present strange contrasts—the subtle wizardry of Leonardo, the simple joyous calm of Raphael, happy-starred youth, the mundane and glowing splendor of Titian, the apocalyptic, power-writhen visions of Michael Angelo.

Of Raphael there has been said enough in these pages to give an idea of the general quality of the man and his works.

Statue of BARTOLOMMEO COLLEONI, the princely condottiere of Bergamo, captain of the forces of Venice. It is the best work of Andrea di Michele di Francesco Cione, called VERROCCHIO, born in or near Florence in 1435, died 1488; goldsmith, bronze founder, architect, painter, sculptor, engineer, musician, and mathematician. The statue was cast after his death by Alessandro Leopardi, who designed the pedestal. Erected about 1493 in the Piazza SS. Giovanni e Paolo, in Venice, it incarnates the greatest qualities bronze has to show.

If frequent reference to him has seemed to place especial emphasis upon him it is merely that he was so normal and so sane and summed up so many excellent qualities that he is a convenient figure to serve as a measure of comparison.

The long span of life that was the lot of Michael Angelo Buonarroti bridges the interval between the Renaissance at its best and in its decadence. From his young manhood in the days of Savonarola in Florence to the suppression of liberty of thought through the Spanish domination that began in 1527 and the introduction of the wickedest engine ever devised for the destruction of mental freedom and personal liberty, the Inquisition, the Italy he loved passed from unfettered thought to the mental shackles of the Catholic Reaction—the reaction of the Church to the Protestant Reformation that was sweeping through the countries of the North. It was his sad fate to see Italian art too decline, and to contribute to that decline, not consciously and deliberately, but, strangely enough, through the very force and power of his work and the mannerisms that crept into it and which a breed of little men mistook for the secret of his mighty genius and tried to borrow that haply they might give distinction to their own stupid concepts.

At sixteen he broke with his master Domenico Ghirlandaio and thenceforth pursued his own path. Obtaining access for study to the gardens of San Marco where Lorenzo de' Medici had installed his fragments of antique art, he attracted the attention of that extraordinary being, was taken into his household, and thereafter until Lorenzo's death he was the companion and intimate of the Magnifico, of Poliziano, Ficino, Pico della Mirandola, and men of like intellect and caliber. Thus his mind was nourished upon all the culture of the day; and his spiritual side responded to the sway of Savonarola then at the height of his power over the

Florentine conscience. When Lorenzo the Magnificent died Angelo fled to Bologna and, after a brief return to Florence, proceeded to Rome, where he was destined to spend the greater part of his life, much of it in the service of the Medici family who debauched and enslaved Florence, whose political policies he bitterly detested, and who yet had placed him under lasting obligation for his start in life and for opportunities adequate to the exercise of even his superlative genius. This relation to the Medici is noted here as one of the controlling factors of his artistic life. We cannot spare the space for many biographical details; his life has been written many times, voluminously and ably. We may note here only the principal lineaments of a life and art that were in very truth but one; he lived only for his art; he never married and lived simply, even meanly, for a man of good birth who was the acknowledged master of the world of art in a time and a city of ostentatious display. He slept little and poorly and often rose while it was yet dark to work by the light of a candle stuck in his cap.

It has been remarked that none of the soft beauty of nature ever appears in his designs, no tree, no blossom, no light of dawn or eventide, but stark rocks only as the bleak and fitting setting for the superhuman shapes that peopled the austere world of his imagination. Adolescence, even childhood, is, with him, muscular. His personages are usually mature, his women like mothers of Titans, his men like Titans themselves. They reflect the travail of soul that seems always to have been his, and his irritations and disappointments seem to live in the moody mien and writhen limbs of the creatures of his sombre fancy. The human body he made plastic to the expression of whatever mood or passion he wished to embody. His painting is like his sculpture in these traits, and his architecture is as plastic as his sculpture, his

Exterior of the CHAPEL OF HENRY VII, the lady chapel of Westminster Abbey, an example of the Late Perpendicular style. Built about 1500, it is interesting to compare with Late French Gothic as at St. Ouen and St. Maclou, Rouen.

The PALAIS DE JUSTICE, in ROUEN, a secular example of Flamboyant Gothic, built from 1499 to 1508. It was upon buildings such as this that the people lavished their effort and treasure when the church-building impulse had waned.

ST. OUEN, in ROUEN, of which this portion was probably built about 1500, is a fine example of the Flamboyant style, into which the Gothic of France developed. Rouen is rich in structures in this style, secular and ecclesiastical.

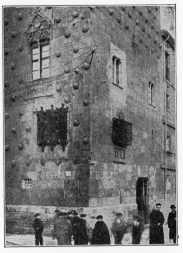

The CASA DE LAS CONCHAS, in Salamanca, Spain. About 1500. Typical of Spanish domestic architecture of the period between Gothic and Renaissance. The small windows barred with wrought iron, and ample wall surfaces, are characteristic.

sculptural conception of architecture as the disposition and modulation of light and shade violating canons held sacred by some of his contemporaries, and leading many followers astray.

In sculpture, his Moses intended for the tomb of Pope Julius II, and the tombs of the Medici in the sacristy of San Lorenzo in Florence; in painting, the vaulted ceiling and the Last Judgment in the Sistine Chapel; in architecture, the dome of Saint Peter's and the buildings of the Capitol in Rome; these are his best-known works.

He died in 1564, at eighty-nine, acclaimed the supreme artist of his epoch, and was laid to rest by reverent hands in the Westminster Abbey of Florence, the Church of Santa Croce.

We may briefly note the short career of Antonio Correggio of Parma, who is a curiously isolated figure in Italian art; apparently he had few or no opportunities for travel or study, but his extraordinary genius triumphed over all such disadvantages; he was a master of chiaroscuro and of draftsmanship, and his color is soft and sweet; his compositions are an ordered riot of joyous and beautiful beings; he had an enormous vogue during the romantic period in English literature, and has been ranked with Angelo, Lionardo, and Raphael, as one of the four greatest artists of Italy. Born in 1494 he was thus contemporary with Michael Angelo, and died at forty, just as Angelo was beginning the Last Judgment.

With the exception of Giorgione, who was born in 1478 and lived but thirty-three years, the three chief figures in the art of painting in Venice belong to the sixteenth century—Titian, Tintoretto, and Veronese. Tiziano Vecello was born the year before Giorgione in the fifteenth century, but he lived and worked for ninety-nine years and the picture-galleries of Europe are glorified by many of the masterpieces of this long and fruitful life. Jacopo Robusti, known as Tintoretto because he was the son of a dyer, dates from 1512 to 1594 and Paolo Cagliari of Verona, always called Veronese, from 1530 to 1588. The Venetian school had had a resplendent history before the advent of these her greatest masters, beginning with Bellini at 1400; but beautiful as the work of that school had been it was chiefly in the general pietistic vein of most Italian painting. It was reserved for this later Venetian school to celebrate the pomps and glories of this world. The time, the lovely city, the sumptuous life of Venice, all conspired to produce a splendid and mundane art full of color and movement. The favorite medium of the Venetians was oil, as fresco was that of the Florentines; and the medium lends itself, in its comparative ease of handling and its certainty of effect, to the rapid decoration of ample spaces.

While Italy was hastening to her decadence elsewhere, here on the bosom of the Venetian lagoons bloomed a late and in many ways the most beautiful flower of the Italian Renaissance. The splendor, the dignity, and the pageantry of Venetian public and private life found in Veronese and Tintoretto their supremely competent celebrants; after the lapse of four centuries their canvases are as modern and fresh in feeling as though painted yesterday. Tintoretto's life-long ambition was to unite the power and force of Michael Angelo's design with the glorious color of the Venetians. The walls and ceilings of the palaces and churches of Venetia glow with the visions of these three masters. They did not devote themselves entirely to secular themes like the Venice Enthroned of Veronese in the Ducal Palace. Titian's Madonna in the Church of the Frari, and Tintoretto's series of religious pictures like those in the Scuola di San Rocco, are among the most noteworthy paintings of their kind

The TOMB OF LORENZO DE' MEDICI, Duke of Urbino (not to be confused with Lorenzo the Magnificent), in the "New Sacristy" of S. Lorenzo in Florence, the family church of the Medici. The entire composition is by MICHAEL ANGELO, executed between 1523 and 1534. In this work and its companion tomb Angelo touches the very summits of his sculptural genius. The seated figure, Lorenzo, is usually referred to as Il Pensieroso, The Thinker. The reclining figures typify Dawn and Twilight.

in the world. But the point of view, the mental attitude of the Venetians, were far removed from that of Michael Angelo, who replied to the peevish complaint of the Pope that there was no gold in the ceiling of the Sistine Chapel, that "these were simple folk, who wore no gold on their garments." And the airy spaces, the wide-winged breezes of the Adriatic, infused a spirit of freedom into Venetian art very different from the cloistral inspiration of the Florentine school. A great religious picture in Venice was an opportunity and a vehicle for the assembly of rich fabrics, vessels of gold and silver, majestic architectural settings, and over all these the magical light of the most beautiful city in the world.

In sculpture Venice was not especially notable—we may mention the Lombardi, Alessandro Leopardi, and Jacopo Sansovino; she floats between her tinted skies and the skies' reflection like the city of a dream; and those skies, tender with the colors of the dawn or piled high with the glories of her jewelled sunsets, turned the thoughts of her artists toward color.

In architecture it is interesting to trace the persistent repetition of the same composition in the Venetian palaces of every period; whether they be Byzantine, Romanesque, Gothic, or Renaissance, they present a similar disposition of voids and solids, the openings grouped in the centre of the façade leaving a space of wall, sometimes blank, sometimes pierced with windows, at each side. Upon every period Venice made her personal impress. To the Byzantine, the Romanesque, Gothic, and Renaissance, she gave a character that makes it Venetian above all. Her architecture is full of color—the soft tones of figured marbles faded to indescribable hues by the sea air and the sun give her buildings a human quality, a friendly warmth, that is all her own. Her intercourse with the East, the tradition of color established early in her history by that jewel-box of the world, the Church of Saint Mark, the proximity of the quarries of creamy Istrian and rose-flushed Verona marbles, all contributed to her effect. Much of Brunelleschi's architecture in Florence, particularly his interiors, executed in a cold gray stone and dead white plaster, is repellent merely because of its sad and dreary color; for, examined as form merely, it is found to be full of a virile and masculine type of charm and beauty. And Rome is fortunate in her wonderful travertine that turns gold with age, in color and texture one of the finest building materials in the world, bestowing upon the Eternal City her cheerful and sympathetic warmth of tone.

Among the architects who gave Venice her Renaissance buildings Jacopo Sansovino easily holds the first place. Born a Florentine, he came to Venice early in life, fell in love with her, acquired citizenship, and is identified with the Venetian rather than the Florentine school. He was a sculptor as well, and the figures which give their name to the Giants' Staircase in the courtyard of the Ducal Palace are his, with the staircase itself. But the building upon which his fame securely rests is the Library on the westerly side of the Piazzetta of Saint Mark, built about 1536. The little church of Santa Maria dei Miracoli, one of the gems of Italy's crown, built by the Lombardi in 1481, exhibits many of the characteristics of the Early Renaissance in Tuscany and elsewhere, and is in essence a belated transitional building.

After the fire of inspiration had burned low, after the creative power had departed from Italy, her architects fell back upon rules and formulas for the confection of masterpieces. To this school of formulists belong Andrea Palladio of Vicenza, Vincenzo Scamozzi of Venice, and Giacomo Barozzi of Bologna and Rome, known as Vignola; and to this group

THE CREATION OF MAN, by MICHAEL ANGELO. A part of the ceiling of the Sistine Chapel, in Rome, begun in 1508 and finished almost without assistance in four and one-half years. "The whole [ceiling] is colored like the dusky, tawny, bluish clouds of thunderstorms. There is no luxury of decorative art here. Sombre and aërial, like shapes condensed from vapor, or dreams begotten by Ixion upon mists of eve or dawn, the phantoms evoked by the sculptor throng that space."—SYMONDS.

MICHAEL   ANGELO   BUONARROTI
Born in Florence, 1475
Died in Rome, 1564

of men and their work, largely because they reduced their formulas to writing and published them, the architects of succeeding generations have unfortunately gone for inspiration rather than to the original Roman and Græco-Roman sources from which the artists of Italy's creative prime derived theirs. But even upon the work of these men Venice had her effect and gave the palaces they built on her canals a *brio* and dash more hers than theirs.

Corresponding to them in point of time are the followers of Michael Angelo, among whom may be noted Giorgio Vasari, almost as famous for his bad architecture and painting as for his immortal Lives of the Painters and Sculptors; also Giulio Romano, Raphael's first assistant, in whom architecture descended to mere rhetoric. Later came Bernini, who built the vast and imposing colonnade around the Piazza of Saint Peter, who was called to Versailles by Louis XIV, and whose posturing and affected angels and saints debase the sky-line of many places in Rome and elsewhere.

The classic inspiration had run its course and at the feet of Michael Angelo the stream divided; one branch led to the frozen region of the formulists, the other plunged over the precipice to the extravagances and meaningless gestures of the Rococo.

After a considerable period of decadence in painting, the Caracci attempted to lead the way to a return to sound principles, and to that end established a sort of academy at Bologna in the latter part of the sixteenth century; their teaching has appreciably affected modern painting through its influence upon the French school. After them the twilight gathers about the art of Italy; against her darkening sky the solitary genius of the Venetian Tiepolo ascends like a signal rocket of farewell and lingers there like a silver star.

CHAPTER XVIII

THE RENAISSANCE PASSES FROM ITALY

Italy's Political and Military Weakness — Louis XI of France and His Claim
to the Kingdom of Naples — Charles VIII and His Invasion — Italy is
Revealed to the Nations of the North — Some Conditions in Europe at
the Opening of the Sixteenth Century — Francis I — He Invites Italian
Artists to France — French Contacts with Italy — Spain and France
Compared — French Sculpture and Painting — The Development of
Renaissance Architecture in France — Art in France from Francis I to
Louis XVI and the Revolution — Louis XIV and the Establishment of
the Academy of Architecture and the School of Fine Arts in Rome —
Official Recognition and Regulation of Art — Louis XV and the Deluge.

THE Renaissance in Italy had completed the appointed
triad—the rapture of its youth, the splendor of its virile
maturity, the weakness and the extravagant affectations of
its decadent old age. The political impotence of the country,
split up as it was into the innumerable petty principalities
and dukedoms which were the fruit of personal ambition
and self-aggrandizement, always centrifugal in their action
and destructive of national unity; the growing wealth of the
middle or burgher class in which the old sturdy sense of independence of the days of the Italian Republics was replaced
by a desire for ease and personal safety: these led to the employment of mercenary soldiers to fight the battles of the
towns. No longer did the citizen seize pike or halberd and
run to the ramparts to defend his city to the death under
the gonfalon of his quarter. Paid captains commanding
bands of hired ruffians recruited from France, Spain, England, Switzerland, and Germany, sold their services to the
highest bidder, and conducted the wars of the cities on a

A portion of the LOUIS XII WING OF THE CHÂTEAU DE BLOIS, a favorite residence of the Kings of France. A work of the Late Gothic period, built early in the sixteenth century, of light stone with panels of light-red brick.

An example of the style current about 1575, in the reign of HENRI III, a pavilion of the Palace of Fontainebleau. The budding Renaissance has lost the grace and beauty of the style of Francis I and is heavy without dignity.

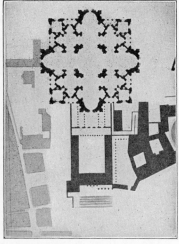

BRAMANTE'S PLAN FOR S. PETER'S, made about 1505. "If he had lived to throw over his mighty masses the golden fabric of his pure and subtle style, it would have been doubtless the most beautiful classic edifice in the world."—H. V. B. M.

Part of the FRANCIS I WING OF THE CHÂTEAU DE BLOIS, the most famous example of the style called by the French "La Renaissance," but properly regarded as transitional. After 1515. It is a beautiful fusion of Gothic and Renaissance motifs.

leisurely plan which shed but little blood and gave ample opportunity for treacherous and profitable accommodation between opposing leaders.

Thus weakened, Italy became the cockpit of Europe and the prey of the nations of the North. It was Louis XI of France who prepared her actual fall; he had laid the explosive train—a claim to the succession of the Kingdom of Naples, which included all of Southern Italy and the Two Sicilies. Ferdinand V of Spain disputed this claim and advanced his own. When Louis died his son succeeded him as Charles VIII, a defective boy of thirteen who took over the government from his able sister, who had acted as Regent, in his twenty-second year, a year notable in the history of the world; the discovery of America and the expulsion of the Moors from Spanish soil in 1492 made Spain rich and powerful and the accession of the incompetent Charles, his feeble brain inflamed with dreams of conquest—these were the immediate events that led to the exploitation of Italy and the spread of her arts and culture to the rest of Europe.

Charles invaded Italy with horse and foot in 1494, reached Naples with no effective opposition, and was forced to retreat to France by the menace of a league that had been formed behind him by Venice as he marched south. With him across the frontier he took sundry Italian artists and artisans of minor rank. The significance of this invasion for the student of art lies in the revelation of the beauty and riches of Italy to the "barbarians," as the French were then called by the cultivated Italians. Once more, after a thousand years, Italy was to ravish the senses and arouse the cupidity of the Northrons; and until the middle of the sixteenth century the Italian soil was to tremble under the shock of foreign battalions fiercely striving for her possession; for the soldiery of Spain and France were no holiday fighters and terrified the Italians grown soft in luxury and the leisurely and bloodless moves of mimic warfare.

We may here conveniently and briefly survey some of the conditions in northern Europe in this period of political and artistic transition. When Charles cracked his poor head against the lintel of a low door at Amboise and died, he was succeeded by Louis XII and he in turn by Francis I in 1515. In 1519 Charles I of Spain fell heir to the vast dominions of the Holy Roman Empire and became the Emperor Charles V, ruler over all of modern Germany and Austria, the Netherlands, Spain, Sicily, Sardinia, and Southern Italy, and all of North and South America west of Brazil. In 1509 Henry VIII became King of England at eighteen. These three were all young kings of about the same age and similar vanity, and the prospects for peace in Europe were small, all being ambitious, Francis careless and fiery, Henry burly and bluff but crafty, Charles a serious religious bigot, endowed with a dull persistence, a stubborn will, and an undershot jaw. Their realms were fairly well consolidated by now and their power practically autocratic. Disunited Italy could not effectively oppose any one of these northern autocrats, although England's part in Italy's fate is negligible except as an indirect force; Henry merely tried to recover some of the provinces of France that had been appanages of the English crown while Francis was engaged in his long and bitter struggle with Charles over the Neapolitan claim.

This struggle took Francis into Italy repeatedly, his tastes were such as to give him some appreciation of Italian art, and he invited numbers of artists to visit France and beautify the new buildings he was constructing or projecting. Lionardo da Vinci, Benvenuto Cellini, Primaticcio, Andrea del Sarto, and Niccolo dell' Abbate, among others, accepted. As early as the middle of the fifteenth century French art-

ST. PETER'S in Rome. The colonnades around the Piazza are by Bernini, the negligible façade by Maderna. The dome is by MICHAEL ANGELO, his crowning architectural achievement. "As one comes down from Tuscany, as he came so often, from the Alban Hills, from the olive-clad slopes of Tivoli or from the sea, the great dome of St. Peter's seems to float like a bubble across the golden reaches of the Campagna, majestic, withdrawn, remote, like the spirit of him who made it."—H. V. B. M.

ists had visited Italy and brought back sketches and impressions; but such contacts under monarchical rule were apt to be sterile; it required the seal of authority of the sovereign and his active interest to give a real impetus to a new form of art.

In France the geographical barriers that fostered the isolation of the Italian cities and the consequent individuality of their arts are lacking; save for the extreme southeastern and southwestern provinces where the spurs of the Alps and the Pyrenees thrust forward, France is one great undulating and gently diversified expanse, so that in all periods her arts have a strong general character that pervades and unites them.

In Spain also there are few physical barriers to national stylization; to all intents and purposes a great tableland whose flanks slope to the Mediterranean and Atlantic shores, here the conformation of the land and the temperature of the seas that beat upon those shores produce wide extremes of climate, and with the long Moorish occupation as a social force modified the arts in detail.

The tendency in France was all toward centralization of power in the hands of the King; the same is true in Spain from the time when Ferdinand and Isabella married and united the provinces of Aragon and Castile; and the whole drift in Europe was toward the monarchy that seemed to promise stability, order, peace, and prosperity, after the chaotic conditions of Feudalism and its snatching and marauding barons.

French and Spanish art came in close contact and in mass contact with the art of Italy in its maturity; they did not seek the original sources which were the founts of Italy's inspiration but drank from the reservoir she had filled through the conduits of her genius. Had the full flood of the classic revival swept France and Spain at the same time as it broke over Italy, the historian and the critic would have a different story to record. It would be intensely interesting to see what each, stirred by the identical impulse, would have made of it, given their racial origins and social traditions. As it was, France had been feudal, a system which was now dying out. Spain had been occupied for centuries by the oriental Moor. Up to the time of Francis I French art was Mediæval, Gothic; the increasing internal security of the times led to a change in the character of the French château and manor-house, and the forbidding Mediæval fortress was to gradually shed its military aspect and its defensive features and become the country house of the gentleman of France. Spain has not had a truly indigenous art, and in her ecclesiastical architecture borrowed freely from France, dipping her borrowed plumes in a tincture of her own. But the strongest single influence in Spanish architecture is that of the Moor and his social customs, at which we have already glanced; it spread from the bare outer walls of his dwellings and their rich interiors and arcaded patios, the tiled and colored domes and minarets of his mosques, to the houses and churches of the Spaniard. So we may find in the same Spanish building, incorporated in the design, not added thereto, Moorish, Gothic, and Renaissance elements— the broad wall spaces of the Moorish occupation, the label mouldings that are relics of the Gothic phase, and the ornamental motifs of the Italian Renaissance. Spanish architecture had a swift decadence in its outer forms in the late Renaissance period; when her artists, always prone to over-emphasis, came under the influence of the Rococo architecture that infested the rest of Europe they presently evolved the Churrigueresque style which for mad and turgid efflorescence cannot be matched in the world.

RAPHAEL'S LOGGIA in the Vatican, looking out upon one of the courtyards designed by his uncle Bramante. It was decorated for Leo X by Raphael and his corps of assistants about 1517–1519 in a new mode, inspired by the then recent discovery of Roman wall decorations in some of the ruined rooms of the Baths of Trajan, at first believed to be grottos—hence the term "grotesque" as applied to this type of decorative detail, in which animal and vegetable forms are interfused and combined.

In France architecture responded first to the call of the Renaissance. In sculpture there existed a strong school of artisans, image-makers rather than sculptors, with a high degree of technical and manual skill—an excellent foundation for the great modern school that was to develop after passing through the insipidities and posturings of the school of Bernini and, much later, under the influence of the frozen inanities of Canova. But in the Early Renaissance in France sculpture occupies a place distinctly dependent upon architecture; it had not yet been submitted to the broader vision, the superior imagination, of the men who were to lift it from the level of a mere craft to that of an art.

Painting had drawn its inspiration from the Netherlands; in fact there were many itinerant Flemish and Dutch painters in France, whose gallicized names conceal their foreign origin; there was no such thing as a really native primitive school as there had been in Italy, so strongly is all early French painting permeated by this foreign influence. That great art of stained and painted glass which is one of the glories of French Gothic did not develop insensibly into a native school of color as we might suppose, due perhaps to the absence of adequate wall surfaces in the churches, and the fortress-like character of the dwellings, whose bare and rough stone walls, unplastered, were concealed by tapestries. Instead of pure painting as mural decoration there was a great deal of painted sculpture which seemed to meet the taste of the time and the conditions of architectural design.

We may therefore most profitably address ourselves to a consideration of the development of Renaissance architecture in France. As in all transitional periods it is in minor details, of ornamentation, of the work around windows and doors, the forms of chimneys, the profiles of mouldings, that we first observe the advent of the new style. The passing of

picturesqueness of the Gothic was slow to yield to the balanced masses and regular spacings of the Classic. And in this combination, of picturesque and clustered masses, of irregular disposition of windows and wall spaces, of high roofs, dormers and chimneys, of all the fundamental structure that was French, with the columns, cornices, and ornamental details of Italy, lay the rudiments of a style that, when the elements were thoroughly interfused, would be as individual as that of Italy. In the reigns of Francis I, of Henri II, III, IV, and Louis XIII, the process of assimilation of Renaissance principles of design continued. The architecture of Italy became completely gallicized by the time of Louis XIV. Modifying details and externals at first, the classic influence penetrated to the structure itself and the very ossature of French architecture became transformed. The lucid and logical French intellect, the intellect of a race of great builders, applied its cool science to the study of Roman and Greek remains as Brunelleschi and Bramante had done before them and evolved from them the modern science of plan, of functional fitness, which the emotional nature of the Italians with their preoccupation with externals, that lack of an innate constructive faculty so remarkable in the heirs of the great structural tradition of the Romans, had failed to develop.

Out of the old Latin alphabet of architecture, the artists of France organized a new language, eloquent, flexible, dignified or playful at will, soundly based upon scientific principles rather than caprice, and containing therefore the principle of growth, of infinite adaptation. Once more art and science met in the same structure to move forward hand in hand to the creation of new beauty in the satisfaction of the demands of modern life. And the Renaissance, revivified, purged of the false rhetoric and excited, over-dramatic gestures of the Italian decadence became the sane expression of civilization.

Let us briefly review some of the architecture that was executed in France from Francis I to Louis XVI.

Francis was a very restless person, constantly moving about from place to place in his realm attended by an immense retinue of splendidly dressed and equipped courtiers with their servants and attendants. Where shelter was not sufficient for this throng of two thousand and upward with horses and dogs, they had to dwell in tents. Hence the enormous hunting-lodges, palatial in extent and character, which Francis built here and there, at Chambord, at Saint Germain, at Fontainebleau. Besides these he added a wing to the royal château at Blois in that silvery valley of the Loire of which he was so fond, and began the modern Louvre in Paris upon the site of an old rendezvous for wolf-hunters called the Louverie.

The names of three architects are identified with the work of this reign: Pierre Lescot, who was the first architect of the new Louvre and served several kings as such; Jean Bullant; and Philibert Delorme who worked at Fontainebleau and the Tuileries in Paris. Among the sculptors who had emerged from the guilds of artisans we may mention Michel Colombe, Germain Pilon, and, the best of his time, Jean Goujon. These men were working side by side with the Italians imported by Francis, not, we may imagine, without heartburnings on the part of the native artists who saw the Renaissance invade France. The Clouets, Flemish artists, were painting the portraits of Francis and his court, while Primaticcio was decorating Fontainebleau, and Lionardo, Cellini, and Andrea del Sarto were also working for the King; but French painters of ability had not yet appeared.

The marriage of Henri II with Catherine de' Medici, a

The PAVILLON HENRI IV at FON-
TAINEBLEAU, retaining the steep roofs of
Mediæval architecture in France and the use,
even in kings' houses, of a combination of
brick and stone. The Renaissance of Italy
was not completely Gallicized in 1610.

The Lower Garden of the VILLA LANTE,
on a hillside at Bagnaia, near Viterbo,
northwest of Rome. Begun 1477, completed
100 years later. One of the most charming of
the Italian Villas. The term Villa embraces
the entire estate, buildings, farm, and gardens.

THE VILLA MEDICI, on the Pincian Hill, in Rome, the home since 1803 of the French
Academy of Fine Arts. Erected toward 1574 by ANNIBALE LIPPI and for a time the
property of the Grand Dukes of Tuscany. Here for four years now live the pensionnaires
of the French Government and, under ideal conditions, study the arts of architecture, painting,
sculpture, music, and engraving, surrounded by all that Rome has to offer of inspiration, of
historical precedent, and of beauty.

daughter of that house which gave two queens to France and two Popes to the Church, reinforced the Italian vogue. Pervaded by Italians, the French court inclined more and more strongly toward Italian manners, Italian dress, Italian art. Catherine de' Medici was the dominating intellect in the reigns of her three sons, who followed their father as Francis II, Charles IX, the hero of the massacre of Saint Bartholomew, and the degenerate Henri III.

When Henri III was stabbed the House of Valois came to an end, and King Henry of Navarre became King of France as Henry IV, the first of the Bourbon dynasty, an able and virile man who governed France well until the dagger of Ravaillac put an end to his gallant life. He was a great builder, and assembled large numbers of artists and artisans of all kinds in the Louvre. His widow, Marie de' Medici, had been brought up in the Palazzo Pitti in Florence, into which her family had moved when Tuscany was made a duchy; when their son Louis XIII married in 1615, Marie bought the place of the Duc de Piney-Luxembourg on the left bank of the Seine and employed Salomon Debrosse to build her the Palais du Luxembourg of to-day; the design is obviously based upon that of the garden front of the Pitti by Ammanati—an instance of direct transplantation of style and motif from one country to another.

The Italian influence at the court of France diminished after the marriage of Louis XIII with Anne of Austria, and when Richelieu came to power France became French again. Armand du Plessis, Cardinal Duc de Richelieu, the minister of Louis and the real ruler of France, was a wise and convinced patron of arts and letters; he established the royal printing-press, founded the French Academy in 1635, and embellished the realm with many important and beautiful monuments, built and decorated in a style that had become thoroughly sophisticated and thoroughly French. And he established the power of the Crown upon a foundation that lasted upward of one hundred and fifty years.

Louis XIII was succeeded by his son Louis XIV, *le Grand*, the Sun King, who reigned in glory for no less than seventy-two years; an able, vain, and pompous little king. He ruled with vigor and prosecuted his wars and administered his internal affairs with equal success; he persecuted the Protestants with similar vigor, many of them artisans of a high type, who, forced to emigrate, carried their arts to England and America. In *Louis le Grand* the power and majesty of the French monarchy culminated in autocracy. He encouraged, established, or re-established all the arts and manufactures that minister to magnificence and luxury. The inherited fiscal policy of Richelieu, relieving the upper classes of taxation at the expense of the lower, made vast sums available for the erection of beautiful buildings filled with tapestries, carpets, carved and gilded furniture, mirrors, porcelains, bronzes, through which moved the courtiers of the King, clad in silks and laces, satins and velvets—an artificial and supercivilized society.

Louis XIV enlarged Versailles from the status of the hunting-lodge that had been a favorite resort of his father to that of the seat of government and the residence of the King and all his court. He employed the French architects Louis Le Vau and J. Hardouin-Mansart, and summoned Bernini up from Rome to consult upon the project. Le Nôtre laid out the superb park and gardens upon the lines of the great *plaisances* of Italy, and Le Brun, the court painter, the King's director of all things artistic, the autocrat in the realm of art, supervised and dictated the work of a throng of painters and sculptors. Louis also added a wing to the Louvre from a design by Claude Perrault, paved the streets

A KNIGHT OF MALTA, by GIORGIONE.
born at Castelfranco near Venice in 1477 and
died in 1510. In Giorgione's youth Lionardo
visited Venice and evidently influenced him
toward rich chiaroscuro. His color is worthy
of the greatest school of color in Europe.

Portrait of SIR RICHARD SOUTH-
WELL by HANS HOLBEIN the Younger,
born at Augsburg in 1497 and died 1543.
In 1525 he went to England and painted
Henry VIII and his Court. A marvellous
draftsman and delineator of character.

The famous PERSEUS by BENVENU-
TO CELLINI, the Florentine goldsmith,
born 1500, died 1571. The account of the
casting of this figure in bronze should be
read, in Cellini's autobiography, by every
student of art, as a vivid human document.

Portrait of FRANÇOIS I, King of France.
The artist is unknown, but the work is evidently that of one of the Teutonic or Flemish
masters, who, like the Clouets, painted in
France in the fifteenth and sixteenth centuries under gallicized names.

of Paris, and built monuments, squares, and arches to celebrate his grandeur.

In his reign, in 1671, the Academy of Architecture and
the School of Fine Arts in Rome were founded—potent
factors in the development of French art, at once pernicious
and beneficial in their results; beneficial in their recognition
of art as a force in the state and society, as contributing to
the glory of a country and a nation, in providing for instruction and in rewarding merit; and pernicious in the stifling
effect of official regulation, and the formulation of arbitrary
standards of taste or manner to which art must conform.
The history of art in France since Richelieu and Louis XIV
is to be read in the sustained conflict between academic
officialdom and its beneficiaries, and the original and progressive architects, painters, and sculptors of France. The
works of Palladio, Vignola, Scamozzi, Serlio, and of old
Vitruvius, authors of architectural cook-books, were undoubtedly in the hands of French architects, and contributed
toward the formulistic tendencies of the whole age.

Religiously, France was as worldly as the monarch and
his court. But after a sufficiently lively life, when the grey
years were closing in about the old King, he came under the
sway of the Widow Scarron, whom he made his morganatic
wife as Madame de Maintenon, and became so devoutly
religious, so suppressed the gaieties of which he had been the
leading spirit, that when he died there was a terrific reaction,
the former royal governess was bundled off, and the reign
of his great-grandchild Louis XV has become a synonym
for gay and cynical corruption. The kingdom was fast
slipping into bankruptcy. The courtesans whom the Regent
and the King maintained as mistresses dominated the scene;
and this corruption and feminist domination of manners
and taste was reflected in the capricious design of the period,

frivolous and perverted as the empty souls that gave it febrile birth.

The reigns of Louis XIV and Louis XV cover a period of one hundred and thirty-one years. They and Richelieu had sown the wind that became the whirlwind to sweep Louis XVI and his Queen and monarchy itself into limbo. The growth of privilege, the heartless and selfish cynicism of the upper classes, the exploitation of the poor, had their just and inevitable sequel in the French Revolution.

CHAPTER XIX

PAINTING AND SCULPTURE IN EUROPE

The Mediæval Art of the North and Advanced Italian Work Contemporane-
ous — Recapitulation of the Traits of the Italian Schools — The Flemish
School — The Spanish — The School of France — The Dutch School —
The Germans — The English — Sculpture in Europe — Goujon — Hou-
don — Rubens — Hals — Poussin — Van Dyck — Velasquez — Claude —
Rembrandt — Ver Meer — Tiepolo — Goya — The Eve of the French
Revolution.

BEFORE we touch upon the great *débâcle* and its effects
upon the orderly movement of artistic progress in the world
we must return to a point from which we may review the
arts of painting and sculpture in Europe. Throughout this
survey we must bear in mind that all Europe outside of
Italy lagged far behind her in culture, particularly the countries where the slower-witted and conservative mind of the
Northerner clung tenaciously to Mediæval thought and custom. Nor was the mind of man reborn there with the rapture that caught the Italians up to such heights of inspired
design. It was as though the Italian spring came slowly
through the northern forests, where the snowbanks of Mediævalism lingered beside the meadows flower-starred by the
Renaissance. Thus we find the Primitives of Flanders and
Germany, essentially Gothic artists in training, tradition,
and vision, contemporaneous with the advanced schools of
Italian painting.

When at last the Renaissance melted the Northern snows,
all Europe turned toward Italy as the authentic source of
warmth and color and intellectual light. The Spaniards
were strongly affected by the Venetian masters, although the

meretricious Caravaggio appealed to some of the sombre predispositions of the Spanish nature. The intellectual point of view of the Caracci of Bologna attracted the French, who seem never to have been drawn to the rich and sensuous warmth of Titian. The great Rubens on the other hand, whom we may esteem as foremost among the Flemings, sought to combine the excellences in composition of the Caracci with those in color of Titian and Tintoretto, and so formed his own style. His pupil Van Dyck carried the Flemish tradition to England, as Holbein had carried the German. Rembrandt, trained solely in the atmosphere of the North, strikes out a path untrodden by any save himself. This little summary will serve to indicate that the narrow bonds of nationalistic isolation were loosed, that Europe was becoming more cosmopolitan and the interactions of art upon art and artist upon artist more and more complex, and the threads of derivation closely intermingled and more difficult to follow. It is impossible for us here to do more than indicate the general characteristics of the principal schools and those of a few of the acknowledged masters.

We have already touched upon the Italian schools and may profitably recapitulate their traits.

The Florentine, sober, balanced, measured, developing from the simple masses and reticent modelling of Giotto to the stupendous creations of Michael Angelo; with a preference for tempera and for fresco; with a certain precision, a definiteness of vision even in the arch-dreamer Angelo who scorns all vagueness, the glamour that lies in the soft fusion of forms and lights and shadows, and who spoke slightingly of Titian's work in oil, holding that it was not a medium for virile men to work in. On the whole an intellectual school, balanced between the things of the mind and those of the spirit.

PRESENTATION OF THE VIRGIN AT THE TEMPLE, painted for the Church of S. Maria dell' Orto in Venice by Jacopo Robusti, called IL TINTORETTO. A painter of terrific vigor and infinite tenderness, his color ranges from the dark and lurid pictures in the Scuola di San Rocco to those exquisite harmonies in silvery gold to be seen in the Ducal Palace. He inscribed these words upon the wall of his studio as the expression of his aspiration: "The color of Titian, the design of Michael Angelo."

Portrait of TINTORETTO by himself
Born at Venice 1518
Died 1594

Of the Roman school we may count Raphael the chief exponent, although he is also grouped with the Umbrians and Florentines—a cosmopolitan school because Rome drew artists to her from all the world; dealing with decorative painting on a large scale, painting portraits incidentally, but chiefly concerned with the celebration of the dogmas and legends of the Church conceived in a worldly vein, or with pagan myth and story, and treating both with equal interest as problems in composition, drawing, and color; boasting no major artist native in Rome, and declining into the empty pomp of Giulio Romano and his fellows.

The soft grace of Perugino, the master of Raphael, is typical of the Umbrian school, whose influence is visible in the ripest achievements of the pupil.

The school of Lombardy or Milan may, for our purpose here, be considered the school of Lionardo; it is distinguished for its lovely chiaroscuro, its subtle interpretation of character, and is content chiefly with surfaces of moderate dimensions upon which could be lavished the treasures of a consummate craftsmanship. Luini is an exemplar of the group.

And lastly the Venetian, a school of oil-painting, of mellow and golden tones in the canvases of Titian and Giorgione, of cool blue and silver, yellow and damask, in Veronese, and of the wide range of the palette of Tintoretto. These Venetians loved the splendor of life, the glory of color, rich compositions that reflected the magnificence of the city whose Doge attended by the Council of Ten and all her noblemen and great ladies went forth each year in state to wed the Sea. The isolation conferred by the lagoons permitted Venetian painting to develop quite independently of the currents of influence that flowed between the other cities of Italy. From Bellini at the birth of the fifteenth century to Tiepolo in the eighteenth, the painting of Venice, like her architecture, is her own, with a deep content in fulness of color; quiet too, if we except the furious energy of Tintoretto. There seems always to be a pause, just as the spectator arrives, in the movement and in the occupations of the personages who throng these canvases, that he may admire their beauty, their poise, the magnificence of their equipage, their simplicity of soul, their joy in merely being.

It was the early school of Venice that influenced the founders of the Flemish school, the brothers Van Eyck, of whom the elder, Hubert, visited the city of the sea. Legend associates their name with the invention of oil-painting, although it is also otherwise ascribed. Hubert was born about 1366 and is known to have gone to Venice toward 1400; whether he learned oil-painting there or carried it with him matters little. The influence of Italian art transpires through the fundamental Flemish quality of the painting of these two brothers, Jan about twenty years the younger. Their meticulous accuracy, that lack of a sense of proportion which lavishes microscopic detail upon the church spire on the horizon, upon every least detail of the landscape, and upon every fact of dress or feature of the figures in the foreground, betrays the Teutonic strain in the Flemish blood, and links them with the miniaturists and illuminators of manuscripts from which the northern schools sprang. The school of Flanders, from these beginnings, became the school of Rubens and Van Dyck who steeped themselves anew in the atmosphere of Venice and yet remained themselves and Flemings. It was a naïvely pietistic school at first, combining the portraiture of the donor of a religious picture, his wife and children, with that of the Holy Family or the representation of sacred story. At its culmination under the brush of Rubens it covered the whole field of painting—vast historical

HILLE BOBBE, a fish-wife of Haarlem, made immortal by that master of characterization and of fresh and vigorous brushwork, FRANS HALS THE YOUNGER, born in Haarlem, Holland, about 1620, and died after 1669. A son and pupil of Frans Hals.

DAVID AT THE CAVE OF ADULLAM, by CLAUDE LORRAINE, born at Chamagne, France, in 1600, died at Rome, where he lived and worked, in 1682. This is only a part of the composition. Claude was the father of landscape painting.

Detail of CASTOR AND POLLUX AND THE DAUGHTERS OF LEUCIPPUS, by PETER PAUL RUBENS, born 1577 and died 1640 at Antwerp. One of the world's ablest painters. This is a characteristically Flemish vision of an incident in Classic story.

Portrait of SIR ANTHONY VAN DYCK by himself. Born at Antwerp in 1599, he died at London at 42 years of age, the most famous pupil of Rubens, and one of the greatest portrait-painters of all time, the founder of the British school of portraiture.

pieces, fantasies, *genre*, portraits, altarpieces, all of a tremendous and controlled vigor; and with Van Dyck, also, passed to noble portraiture. The tapestries of Flanders have always been famous and were a stimulus to design on a large scale; Rubens contributed many cartoons to the Flemish looms.

The art of Spain is linked to that of the Netherlands and Italy; until Velasquez, Spanish art as a whole and especially painting, exhibits a morbid and agonized religiosity; the tender heart of the Virgin is pierced with many swords, tears stream from her eyes, tears bedew the cheeks of the attendant saints, not one quiver of the crucified Christ is spared us. The Spanish temperament, prone to extremes, found the works of Correggio and Caravaggio sympathetic, influencing such men of power and ability as Ribera and Zurbaran. When Velasquez came, and "dipped his brush in light and air" he drew to himself all the virtues of the school and dominates the Spanish scene. Not even the insipid sentimentalities of Murillo nor the astigmatic and contorted crudities of El Greco can mar that glory.

Between the Flemish and the Spanish school lay that of France, which, as previously indicated, had no real existence as a native school until the seventeenth century and which then was inspired by the principles taught in the Academy conducted by Lodovico Caracci in Bologna from 1589, by the work of Correggio, and by the classical influence of Poussin. It is somewhat surprising upon glancing at the map of Europe to see France at this time as a colorless island surrounded by great and vigorous schools of painting.

The Dutch school, close as it was physically to that of Flanders, was spiritually far away. It was a Protestant art and did not deal with pietistic compositions for churches; it was a great school of *genre*, of portraiture, of still life, of landscape, painted usually at a small scale for dwellings of modest size; we may except the great group portraits of the guilds and companies of merchants, popular in Flanders also. It gave birth to two such supreme masters as Ver Meer and Rembrandt, widely disparate in vision and method.

The Germans remained inveterately Gothic and Teutonic until far into the Renaissance. Although Albrecht Dürer, perhaps their best man, lived on the highroad to Italy, although he crossed the Alps and made a long stay there, he remained invincibly German and Mediæval despite the fact too that he lived and worked at the very apogee of the Italian Renaissance. Hans Holbein has less of this strong Teutonic flavor, due perhaps to his long residence in England from 1525.

As to the English school, it derives from Van Dyck the Fleming, Holbein the German, and Claude de Lorraine the Frenchman, and owes little directly to the painters of Italy. We are deferring the consideration of the Renaissance in England to a later chapter.

Sculpture in Europe after Michael Angelo was very feeble. Nowhere does it rise above the level of mere good craftsmanship as that may be interpreted to mean good technique; and it frequently falls below that standard. Next after architecture, painting was the leading art. Sculpture, following in its train and adopting the pictorial point of view, lost itself in details, in the effort to express ideas and emotions which lie beyond its proper domain; it was trivial and therefore negligible in this general summary. Spain, Germany, the Netherlands, England—in none of these countries do I find anything really significant in sculpture until recent years; nor in France, with the exception of Jean Goujon, until Clodion and Houdon. When Colbert became Intendant for Louis XIV he found that he would have to train

*VENICE ENTHRONED, painted upon the ceiling of the Hall of the Great Council in the Doge's Palace, by Paolo Cagliari, known as VERONESE from the city of Verona, where he was born in 1528. He died, probably in Venice, in 1588. One of the incidents of his life was his trial before an ecclesiastical court for alleged impiety in introducing monkeys and buffoons among the spectators in religious compositions. "Veronese elevated pageantry to the height of serious art."—*SYMONDS.

sculptors and painters for the many works set afoot in the kingdom, notably at Versailles; this he accomplished in part by the School of Fine Arts at Paris and at Rome. Among the many artists so trained we may distinguish the sculptors Germain Pilon, Puget, and Coysevox. The sculpture of this time lacks the inner beauty, the restraint, and the lofty vision of great art, be it Greek, Mediæval French, or Italian Renaissance; it was pleasing and agreeable frequently, but its air of conscious elegance robbed it of the beauty that lies in the simple and unconscious. Clodion and Houdon, who bridge the chasm between the monarchical world before the Revolution and the republican and Imperial world that followed it, both have charm and character, and Houdon is entitled to the first place among the sculptors France produced until her modern school arose; his portrait of Voltaire would alone proclaim him a master in the field to which his talent and the spirit of his time confined his successes.

Some brief biographical notes upon the artists of Europe from the Early Renaissance in France to the Revolution will complete this portion of our study. The steadily increasing freedom of intercourse between all the countries of Europe gave the artists of this later Renaissance a measure of cosmopolitanism; the narrow barriers of local schools no longer confined their horizons; hence we may let them pass before us in their chronological order, rather than group them under the ensigns of their schools.

The first figure is that of Peter Paul Rubens, who was born in 1577 and in whose tranquil life success followed easily upon success; until his death in 1640 he was not merely a painter of enormous fecundity of invention and accomplishment, but a travelled and cultivated man of the world; everything he did seemed to be done without effort, whether it was to paint a series of immense pictures for the Dowager Queen of France, Marie de' Medici, or conduct the delicate negotiations that led to peace between Spain and England. His early studies led him to Italy where he seems to have absorbed just as much of the great qualities of the Venetian and Bolognese schools as he needed, his calm Flemish temperament permitting him to remain quite himself. This was not his only visit to Italy; his diplomatic duties took him to the ducal court of Mantua as well as to the royal houses of Spain, France, and England.

His work ranged from the Descent from the Cross to A Lion Hunt, through portraiture, historical paintings, altar-pieces, and the depiction of official pageantry. His palette was simple in the extreme and yet he achieves an effect of extraordinary richness and variety. One of the characteristics of his work is the abounding vigor which, upon study, is seen to be always under the strictest control, giving the effect of improvisation, but every line and tone calculated with the calm science that underlay the art of the man.

Frans Hals was a very different sort of person. He is one of the leading men of the Dutch school; born in 1584 he lived to the good old age of eighty-two and in his early life was something of a roisterer, frequenter of taverns, even a toper—which did not prevent his being duly honored as an artist in his own time, nor from being one of the most accomplished portrait-painters and masters of brushwork in Europe.

In 1594 Nicolas Poussin was born, the man who founded the French school of painting. His early training was, as we might expect from the antecedents of French painting, Flemish. But he went to Rome and thereafter could with difficulty be persuaded to leave the city where he found his inspiration. After the little pictures in which the figures of

THE SURRENDER OF BREDA, painted between 1645 and 1648; known also as The Lances. This masterpiece of the middle life of VELASQUEZ is now in the Prado Museum, in Madrid, Spain. He was a contemporary of Rembrandt, Rubens, and Van Dyck. It was a golden age in the art of painting when this wonderful group of artists were all at work.

Self Portrait by
DON DIEGO RODRIGUEZ DE SILVA y VELASQUEZ
Born at Seville, 1599
Died at Madrid, 1660

classical mythology play out the ancient myths in a landscape setting half decorative and theatrical had made him
famous in France, Louis XIII called him back to Paris,
which was beginning to take an interest in Roman antiquity.
He was made First Painter in Ordinary, but he longed for
his beloved Rome, went back to her as soon as he could, and
passed away in 1665. From him the painting of France
takes a new turn, soon to be truly national.

Contemporary with Poussin is the great pupil of Rubens,
Anton Van Dyck. After working under Rubens he took the
road to the artists' Mecca, Italy, already at the age of
twenty-two an accomplished painter; for four years he travelled and in that time painted the portraits of over fifty
notables. Titian and Tintoretto made their impress upon
him, but, like Rubens, he remained himself. Although he
painted altarpieces and similar ideal compositions he was
of all things a superlative painter of portraits. Passing over
to England, where he painted Charles I and was knighted by
him, he remained there, and the private galleries of England
alone contain over three hundred and fifty of his works. A
courtly gentleman, his vision simple, serious, quiet, distinguished, he was the ideal recorder of the society of Europe.
His color is sober and he deals with black, white, and gray
as only great painters can; and the florid and opulent vulgarity that spoils so much of his master Rubens's work is
entirely absent. Born in 1599 he lived but forty-two years.
His painting had an immense effect upon the admirable portrait school that soon sprang up and flourished in England.

The years that usher in the seventeenth century are rich
in the birthdays of great figures in the world of painting.
In the same year as Van Dyck the master known as Velasquez, Don Diego Velasquez de Silva, was born in Seville.
One of his early masters was Ribera, and he married the

daughter of another, Pacheco, upon whose recommendation he went to seek his fortune in Madrid, where he came in contact with the many canvases by Titian owned by the royal family, and painted Philip IV and his brother. At the Spanish court he met Rubens who urged him to go to Italy, where the Venetians threw open to him the magical world of light and color. From then on his life is but the tale of the unfolding of his suave but prodigious genius. He is the peer of any painter in the world in everything that makes a painter; his color has not the splendor of the Venetians, for the Spanish court clothed itself in black; Velasquez is the interpreter of the restraint and austerity that was a part of the finer elements of the Spanish character; he is the painter of light and air, of the quaintness of princely children, of the grotesque in the swarms of dwarfs the King maintained, and of the dignity and gravity of age and of the Kings of Spain, their Grandees and Admirals. To everything he touched he gave the distinction that was Velasquez. Akin to Rembrandt in his artistic qualities, he never knew the vicissitudes that saddened the life of his great Dutch contemporary, and died in honored and honorable ease in Madrid in 1660.

Another contemporary of Velasquez, Rembrandt, Van Dyck, and Poussin, was Claude de Lorraine, whose patronymic was Gellée, and in whose case the particle "de" indicates his place of origin, not noble birth, for the young Claude was a pastry-cook and went to Italy in that capacity. Here his real vocation declared itself and he became one of the most noted landscapists in the history of art, the founder of the modern landscape school. It is a curious thing that landscape in and for itself had not appealed to painters before Claude. In the pictures of the Italians and Flemings it is frequently utilized as a background or setting, but treated

The picture known as *THE NIGHT WATCH*, by *REMBRANDT VAN RIJN*, now in the Ryks Museum in Amsterdam, painted in 1642 for Captain Frans Banning and his company of militia. Rembrandt's work is immensely varied in character, even in contemporaneous works, but Walter Armstrong has said of him, "the one thing in which he never varies is loyalty to his own gift." The greatest etcher and one of the greatest painters the world has known.

Self Portrait by
REMBRANDT VAN RIJN
Born in Leyden, 1606
Died at Amsterdam, 1660

conventionally with a decorative intent, as a piece of tapestry might be hung up behind the personage or action portrayed. But the beauty of landscape, the glamour of dawn and the waning day, the forms of cloud and tree, and the magic of light falling on hill or plain or the wide reaches of waters, had never appealed to artists until Claude came. His pictures often bear the titles of Classical story, but the figures that justify the titles are so small and so subordinated that they merely give life and scale to the scene in which they move. For eighty-two years, from 1600, he taught the French and through them the rest of the world to see landscape as worthy of loving interpretation.

Six years later than Claude, that is to say in 1606, there was born in Holland in the city of Leyden one of the greatest artists the modern world has known; Rembrandt van Rijn is worthy to stand with Michael Angelo, Shakspere, and Beethoven as a kindred soul. Much of his life is veiled in obscurity; he had no marked professional antecedents and he left no definite artistic posterity. When he was about fifty years old it would seem that he lost everything he possessed; just how is not clear; and from then on until his death at sixty-three he would appear to have led a life of comfortless flitting from abode to abode until he obscurely died—a pathetic ending for the artist whose work is one of the glories of the world. He was entirely uninfluenced by Italian art and his point of view and technique became, as they developed and ripened, absolutely personal. In tone his early period resembles the current trend of the Netherlands, gray and black and brown, but deepens and richens with the passage of years into a system of strong concentration of light and massing of warm, transparent, and luminous shadow, handled with masterly freedom of the brush. He was the greatest etcher who has ever held the needle; whatever his genius wrought upon was transfigured; the Jews and the fusty old women of Amsterdam are raised by his touch to a place among the immortals. So may the nobility of the artist's vision lift the poor, the lowly, even the sordid, to that plane where all things are equal if the beauty in them is divined.

Of Johannes or Jan Ver Meer of Delft there is little known except his exquisite work; that he was born in 1632 and that he died young, in 1675, is established. Less than forty paintings are ascribed to him with authority, all small, all bathed in atmosphere, all marvellous in craftsmanship, in the rendition of textures, in perfection of surface, in impeccable draftsmanship. Simple themes—a young woman in a yellow jacket opening a casement, a map on the wall behind her, some household objects on a table covered with an eastern rug—but all metamorphosed, given a new meaning, a new beauty by the magic of the painter's vision.

The closing years of the seventeenth century gave Giambattista Tiepolo to the world. The school of Venice, like all the Italian schools, had fallen into desuetude when this sprightly genius was born in Venice and born a painter, formed later upon Titian, Tintoretto, and Veronese. He travelled much, went up into Germany, and was called to Spain by Charles III. In the seventy-four years of his life his production was immense, peopling the walls and domes of Italy with his airy fantasies. It mattered little whether the theme were religious or not; the characters of Christian or of pagan allegory floated with equal ease and in equal beauty against the tender blue of Tiepolo's skies and the delicate grays and pearly whites of their clouds. He knew how to assemble the pomp of a festival as Veronese had known, and deals in cool tones that are never chalky and have a richness that is always light.

*THE EMBARKATION OF ANTONY AND CLEOPATRA, by GIOVANNI BAT-
TISTA TIEPOLO, born at Venice in 1696 and died at Madrid, Spain, in 1770. This
mural painting is one of several in the Salone of the Palazzo Labia, in Venice, in which Tiepolo painted an architectural framework of columns and arches, through which these splendid pageants are seen. It is a mark of the period that the heroes and heroines of Classic
story are clothed in the dress of the Renaissance.*

In Spanish art the last important figure of the period is that of Goya—Goya y Lucientes—a painter of power, range, and individuality. He, like so many of these others, visited Italy, but said long afterward that he owed all he became to Rembrandt, Velasquez, and nature. He was a very gay young man and threw himself into all the frivolities of the time of Charles III of Spain. Later in life, when Spain was disturbed by revolt, he became serious and sardonic and satirized Spanish life and character in groups of drawings and etchings that are vitriolic in their savage irony. His productive life ended at eighty-two in Bordeaux, 1828.

With this brief account of some of the major figures of Continental painting we approach the eve of the Revolution in France in which the Rights of Man grappled with Privilege of Birth and the Divine Right of Kings and, encouraged by the success of the American Revolution, changed the course of history and checked for a time the natural issues of the Renaissance.

For nearly two centuries in France the Third Estate—all that part of the nation neither noble nor clerical—had had no voice in the government of the country; manufacturer, merchant, professional man, artisan, farmer, all were heavily taxed and saw their hard-won money poured into the laps of spendthrift courtesans, or dissipated in royal and courtly display, in all the ways that pandered to the extravagant tastes of a dissolute King and a corrupt court. And in spite of huge revenues, by the time Louis XVI succeeded to his grandfather's throne the Crown was almost bankrupt.

With the accession of Louis XVI and his Austrian Queen, Marie Antoinette, there was a distinct amelioration of manners and morals. These were good sovereigns as rulers went, Louis weak and Marie Antoinette unwilling to accept the suggestions of economy and retrenchment urged upon the pair by the King's ministers. Followed a series of loans floated at ruinous rates of interest, until the Minister of Finance in despair advised the convocation of the States General, an assembly of the three Estates, the nobility, the clergy, and the commons, the first of its kind in one hundred and seventy-five years. This gathering proved to be of a very different timber and temper from the servile assemblies into which Louis XIV had been wont to stalk in riding dress, and order the registration of his decrees, whip in hand. The entire middle class, particularly the professional elements and especially the lawyers, had developed immensely intellectually and morally and had definite notions upon the Rights of Man. The American Revolution, in which the young Republic had the generous support and encouragement of all the best in France, a revolution based on the proposition that all men are created free and equal, had greatly encouraged all those Frenchmen of vision to whom the conditions in France, social and political, were a cause of offense and loathing. The oppressions of the noblesse with their rights of life and death and castigation over the bodies of their peasants—relics of that Feudalism so highly praised as a social system in some quarters—the overwhelming taxes, the extravagance, profligacy, and worthlessness of the nobility as a class, had kindled deep down in the souls of the people a hot and sullen resentment that smouldered until the convocation of the States General gave it outlet and fanned it into flame, to consume the monarchy and burn up much that was good along with the hideous abuses it destroyed in its wrath. In this terrible eruption, comparable with that which has stricken Russia since the World War, the lowest dregs of the population were thrown to the surface and in their mad lust to revenge the wrongs of centuries wreaked their fury upon the innocent and the guilty alike;

A Chapel Enclosure of the reign of LOUIS XIII at Fontain bleau, indicating the architectural details of an interior of his period, usually painted in several light tones with gilded ornament and mouldings, and showi g a growing mastery of Renaissance design.

Part of the EASTERLY FAÇADE OF THE LOUVRE, designed for Louis XIV by CLAUDE PERRAULT. The Italian mode had been completely assimilated and the architecture of France was by then thoroughly French, dignified, sometimes pompous.

The PALAZZO PESARO, on the Grand Canal, an example of the vigorous late Renaissance palaces of Venice in which was perpetuated the disposition of windows and wall spaces of the earliest days. Built by LONGHENA in 1679, finished in 1710.

The SALLE DU CONSEIL in the Palace of Fontainebleau, of the Period LOUIS XV, decorated by Boucher, Vanloo, and Pierre, expressing in its luxuriant ornateness the taste of the Monarch and his Court. An inappropriate setting for the life of to-day.

and among their victims Louis XVI and his Queen paid for the sins of his fathers under the triangular blade of the guillotine.

The tastes of the King and Queen had been quiet, orderly, and refined, and the *Style Louis Seize* gave promise of leading the way to the highest level the Renaissance had ever reached, an art at once reasoned, structural, and beautiful. But with the Revolution the thought of the day was directed, not forward strangely enough, but backward to the virtues, real or imagined, of the Roman Republic, and a reversion to what was believed to be Classical taste supervened in dress, in furniture, in architecture in a moderate degree, and in painting; a reversion which sharply checked the normal progress of the Renaissance. With the Directorate and with Napoleon, came in the pseudo-classic *Directoire* and *Empire* styles, empty and factitious galvanization of classic forms and ornament, sprung from no native taste or national roots, in which stiff and awkward angularity and heaviness masqueraded as Grecian grace and Roman power.

Of this period in painting Louis David may be taken as the type; his design inspired by classical bas-reliefs, his color dull, livid, pallid, and cold—cold as the heart of the man who could calmly sketch his unfortunate Queen from a window as she passed in the tumbril, forsaken, insulted, to the blood-stained scaffold in the *Place Louis Quinze*.

CHAPTER XX

THE RENAISSANCE IN ENGLAND AND
THE AMERICAN COLONIES

The Renaissance Comes Late to England — The Tudor Transition — Literature the English Contribution to the Renaissance Movement — English Contacts with Italy — Inigo Jones — Sir Christopher Wren and Others — Hogarth — Reynolds — Gainsborough — Raeburn — Romney — Cosway — Old Crome — Constable — Turner — The Renaissance Crosses the Atlantic.

THE English Channel was just wide enough to check the rapid spread of Continental influences and to delay England's immediate participation in the successive developments of Continental art, just as the Alps had interposed their physical barrier to the immediate flow of Italian art into neighboring lands. The Renaissance therefore came very late to England; while her insularity has permitted her to give a certain local accent to the arts she has borrowed from abroad, she has paid the price of isolation in a considerable measure of provinciality and weakness. The conservatism of the Briton, his determination to be British above all things, have militated against the easy absorption of new ideas whether foreign or domestic. British arts like other British things are slow to change, although the physical geography of England lends itself to the ready interchange of ideas between all her shires. And Scotland early presents some interesting variants due to her long and sympathetic relations with France.

The transition from Mediævalism to the Renaissance in England marches with the crescent strength and final consolidation of the power of the Tudor line in the reign of

ST. PAUL'S, LONDON, the principal work of Renaissance architecture in England, designed by her greatest architect, SIR CHRISTOPHER WREN: built between 1675 and 1710 and undoubtedly his masterpiece. It betrays the influence upon Wren of the work going on in Paris under Louis XIV and seems to owe more in detail to France than to Italy. The undue length of the nave repeats the gravest fault of St. Peter's; they are nevertheless the two greatest modern temples in Christendom.

Henry VIII, when the arts of Italy were imported through Flemish and German agencies; in the style which resulted, the Tudor Style, the unlovely Teutonic and Flemish versions of Italian design were grafted on to the English Perpendicular stock—a very imperfect union.

When the bitter struggle between Henry VIII and the Papacy resulted in the separation of the English church from Rome and a Protestant England; when English enterprise awoke under Henry's able daughter Elizabeth; when Drake and Raleigh and a host of other English seamen began to harry the Spaniard, seize his plate ships, raid his treasure towns on the Spanish Main, and at last, falling upon the Great Armada he had dedicated to the conquest of Britain, scattered it to the winds and broke his power upon the sea, England became the dominant maritime nation of the world; when in her turn she began to explore and to colonize; when security and wealth came to her; then England's Renaissance began. Neither in architecture, in painting, nor in sculpture did she produce essentially new things; just as her design, in the Gothic architecture built by Englishmen themselves— not by the visiting master builders from France who built the best Gothic she has to show—fails to grasp the true significance of Gothic, so her arts in the Renaissance are merely such variants of the forms transmitted by Italy, France, and Flanders, as could be expected of a nation non-creative in all the arts save literature. Here was England's real contribution to that vast humanistic movement we call the Renaissance; as Italy's had been painting and sculpture and in the eighteenth century was to be music; and as France's was rationalized architectural design. Even here, in the drama of the great Elizabethans, Italy made herself felt— in plot, in scene, in the dreadful fascination she exercised over the imagination of English writers as a land of intrigue and mysterious death, of stiletto and poison, of strange loves and stranger passions.

English contacts with Italy grew more and more frequent and Italian artisans began to replace Germans and Flemings. Then, in 1573, came Inigo Jones, who went down into Italy toward the close of the sixteenth century and studied her architecture at first hand. He fell at once, in North Italy, under the spell of Palladio, who had but recently died. When he came back he transformed the architecture of England by directing the thought of her architects into another and clearer channel than that clogged by the Teutonries which had been their inspiration theretofore. Every trace of Gothic disappears. Jones was a talented architect, but he appeared at an unfortunate moment, in the decadence of Italian Renaissance architecture, when the essential tranquillity and simplicity of the classical spirit was disturbed and obscured by sixteenth-century ineptitudes.

Between Jones and Wren there is a notable absence of strong designers from the English scene. Christopher Wren was born in 1632 and died, the greatest architect of England's Renaissance, in 1723. At the age of twenty-nine he was a Fellow of All Souls' College, Oxford, an astronomer of repute, and as a mathematician was appointed an Assistant Surveyor-General of Works. His first essay in the field of architecture was in Oxford, but five years later the Great Fire of London swept clear an immense field for the exercise of his talents. He not only made a new plan on modern lines for a new London—unhappily never carried out—but built many beautiful churches including the crowning achievement of his career, Saint Paul's Cathedral. The influence of the new works going on in Paris under Louis XIV, which he studied in person, is plainly visible in Wren's work, which owes more to French than to Italian models.

THE RT. HON. LADY ELIZABETH
COMPTON, painted by SIR JOSHUA
REYNOLDS, the first President of the
Royal Academy, knighted by George III
upon his election, born in 1723 at Plympton,
in Devonshire, died at London in 1792.

YOUNG WOMAN OPENING A CASE-
MENT. by JAN VER MEER, born at
Delft, Holland, in 1632, died there about
1675. A favorite color scheme of this greatest
of the Little Masters—yellow bodice, dark
blue skirt, grey wall, deep red in small masses.

THE SHRIMP GIRL. by WILLIAM
HOGARTH, born at London, 1697; he died
there in 1764; the first of a truly native line
of artists in Great Britain. This picture is
different in type from any other of his works,
usually of a moralistic type.

Portrait of DON SEBASTIAN MAR-
TINEZ by FRANCISCO JOSÉ GOYA,
born, 1746, at Fuentetodos, near Saragoza,
Spain, died at Bordeaux, France, 1828. This
simple and distinguished portrait indicates
one aspect of the work of this many-sided man.

The ritual of the Church of England, with the participation by the congregation in the service, materially affected the interior arrangements and character of new Protestant churches; they had to be light enough that the congregation might see to read the Book of Common Prayer and be of a shape and size that would make the sermon audible everywhere. Those which Wren and his pupils and successors built have established a type that has long prevailed in the design of Protestant churches, even those of Dissenting sects, and which reacted to a certain degree upon that of the churches built during the Gothic revivals which occur from time to time. Some of these successors were Nicholas Hawksmoor, Gibbs, Vanbrugh, and Sir William Chambers. Later came the brothers Adam—one of whom, Robert, visited Rome and was a friend of Piranesi, then at the summit of his fame as an etcher of antique subjects—who represented in England the Classical reaction to which Stuart and Revett's book on the Antiquities of Athens contributed strongly, expressed in France by the Directoire and Empire styles of Percier and Fontaine.

In all this long term of years not one sculptor of quality is to be noted, with the possible exception of Grinling Gibbons, better known as an ornamentist than a sculptor.

For painting there is far more to record. We have already spoken of Holbein, whose intensely personal genius left but little impress upon English art, and of Van Dyck, whose influence was immense and whose supple spirit adapted itself to that of the English social atmosphere. The English school of painting is substantially a brilliant school of portraiture, distinguished by the names of Hogarth, Sir Joshua Reynolds, Gainsborough, Romney, Hoppner, Sir Henry Raeburn, and Sir Thomas Lawrence. Of these, Hogarth, earliest in point of time—1697 to 1764—struck the first national note in British painting. The works by which he was best known for years, indeed those with which the name of Hogarth is chiefly associated even to-day, were the pictures in which he satirized conditions of English life, such as the Rake's Progress, and which were engraved and widely distributed. In these we have Hogarth the moralist; but there is another and more agreeable Hogarth who transpires in such portraits as the Shrimp Girl.

So long as English is spoken we may suppose Sir Joshua Reynolds and Thomas Gainsborough will be acclaimed in England as the bright stars of her artistic firmament, although Raeburn outshines them by far, and George Romney is nearly as able as they. Reynolds was born in 1723 and died in 1792, was President of the Royal Academy with all the prestige of that exalted post, and wrote much, sometimes wisely, upon art. With all his pseudo-science he was a poor craftsman and many of his pictures have cracked, faded, or otherwise deteriorated. Gainsborough falls within the span of Reynolds' life—1727 to 1788—and like him was a various painter; his manner was exceedingly tight in his earlier work, but gained in freedom as he grew older. The positions allotted to these two men in the hierarchy of art by English criticism could only have been possible in a country or at a time deficient in much strong rival talent. It has also been the fashion to decry the work of Sir Thomas Lawrence, who is in many ways a more distinguished painter than either. But in all these matters the student of art should strip himself of all prejudice and, untrammelled by second-hand opinions, judge for himself, fearlessly make up his own mind—and with equal courage change his mind if new light upon the matter in question warrants it.

Henry Raeburn, born in Scotland in 1756 and knighted by George IV in 1822, is at once one of the soundest and

Portrait Statue of VOLTAIRE, the French philosopher, dramatist, historian, and satirist, by JEAN ANTOINE HOUDON, born in 1741 and died in 1828. This amazing portrait of the aged cynic now stands in the foyer of the Comédie Française in Paris.

REV. WILLIAM PENNICOTT, by SIR THOMAS LAWRENCE, born at Bristol, England, in 1769 and died at London in 1830. He succeeded Sir Joshua Reynolds as Painter-in-Ordinary to the King, and was elected President of the Royal Academy in 1820.

WILLIAM FORSYTH, by SIR HENRY RAEBURN, one of the greatest painters Great Britain has produced. A fine example of this master of portraiture. Raeburn was born, in 1756, at Stockbridge, near Edinboro, in which city he died in 1823.

One of a pair of SEATED LIONS flanking the "Emperor's Gate" of the Palace of the Tuileries, in Paris. By ANTOINE-LOUIS BARYE, born in Paris, 1796, and died there, 1875. He has been called the Michael Angelo of the animal world.

most brilliant painters of whom Britain can boast. He was apprenticed in his boyhood as so many great Italian painters were, to a goldsmith, but turned soon to painting; his bent was portraiture and he was far beyond his day and country in the soundness and directness of his technique, a technique amazingly modern in quality, anticipating that freedom of handling we are made familiar with by that great modern master of brushwork, John Singer Sargent. He had very little formal training and left his native country only thrice, one of these occasions being a journey to Italy of some two years' duration, when he was about forty-four. His portraits of men have strength, those of his women grace and beauty, and all of them have character. His color is warm and sympathetic. I cannot recall a single insipid canvas by Raeburn, and in such portraits as that of The MacNab he rises to the level of the greatest portraiture the world possesses.

George Romney was more of the votary and celebrant of famous beauties. His ability, like Raeburn's, was largely native and self-trained. His pictures aside from portraiture are now forgotten, but he painted some of the best-known and most highly prized portraits of the English school. He born in 1734 and died in 1774.

No school of miniature painting excels the English; it is an offshoot of the portrait school, and Cosway and Cooper are the leading figures of the group.

English painting has never been strong in complex figure compositions; in Roman Catholic countries there was always a stimulus to work in that kind, in altarpieces and the like; and at the height of the interest in the themes of antiquity, mythological subjects were in vogue in Italy. Protestant England, like Protestant Holland, fell back upon portraiture, *genre*, and landscape.

Of English landscape-painters we may particularize Joh*
Crome—Old Crome—who was born in the same year a*
Lawrence, 1769, and died in 1821; Constable, who was bor*
in the year of American Independence and lived until 183*
and whose work strongly affected French landscape-paintin*
after the exhibition of his work in Paris in 1824–1825; an*
J. M. W. Turner, born in 1775, an eccentric genius whos*
knowledge of the structure of rocks and hills and tree form*
was profound and who was interested, long before the Im*
pressionists appeared, in the painting of light; who died i*
1851 leaving his unsold works to the British nation; and wh*
left no school and no strong impress upon the artistic though*
of the world, despite the extravagant praise accorded him b*
that least trustworthy of all critics of art, John Ruskin.

.   .   .   .

The countries of the Old World transmitted to thei*
colonies in the New forms familiar to the colonists who modi*
fied them to meet the conditions of climate or the material*
they found in their new homes. Spain gave her architectur*
to Cuba, Porto Rico, Florida, and Mexico; Canada repro*
duced the gray stone architecture of France; Holland'*
children brought with them the roofs, stoeps, and gable*
still to be found on Long Island and in the valleys of th*
Hackensack and the Hudson; but English architectural tra*
dition naturally prevails, for the English capture of New Am*
sterdam substituted English taste for Dutch in New York*
the settlements of Massachusetts, Rhode Island, Connecti*
cut, Virginia, Maryland, and the Carolinas, gave the entir*
Atlantic seaboard English customs, traditions, and arts*
and when England superseded France politically in Canada*
the architecture of the Canadian provinces was measurably
affected. In the old French city of New Orleans, the seaport
of the vast hinterland that was Louisiana, the traditions of

INDEPENDENCE HALL, Philadelphia, one of the best examples of the Colonial Style in America, built in 1729. Built of red brick trimmed with white, its strong masculine quality is quite different from that of the domestic work of the period.

LE PETIT TRIANON, at Versailles, the favorite residence of Marie Antoinette. Although erected from the designs of GABRIEL in the last years of the reign of Louis XV it is accounted a work of the Louis XVI epoch.

THE LOUVRE AND THE TUILERIES. In 1527 François I tore down an old rendezvous for wolf-hunters called the Louverie, and began the structure which became the residence in Paris of the rulers of France, and which they all took pride in extending and embellishing. PIERRE LESCAUT was the first architect employed upon it, and to name the artists who since have wrought upon it is to call the roll of France's artistic glory. The portion called the Palace of the Tuileries was partially destroyed in 1870–1871.

France mingled and often fused with Spanish motifs, with charming results.

Although there were many colonies in North America, the style that is known in the United States as Colonial is of English origin, a child of the English-Renaissance, a descendant of the art of Italy. In England its immediate predecessors or contemporaries are known as Georgian, named from the German Georges who through the humorous fortunes of royal succession so long occupied the English throne. This Colonial Style is in essence a wooden architecture, or wood and brick and occasionally wood and stone in combination. Wood was plentiful, stone and brick difficult to quarry, make, or import. So that the cornices and columns that in England are usually of stone and of stone proportions and dimensions, in America were translated into wood, and in translation became more delicate in scale and assumed aspects in harmony with the limitations and qualities of the material. The style is by no means uniform through all the colonies. It is prim and severe where the Puritan laid his icy hand, grave and sturdy in the Philadelphia of the Quaker, genial and homelike in Maryland and Virginia where the social atmosphere was more Cavalier than Roundhead.

In painting, the American names of note in this early time are Copley, Stuart, and West. Copley would never have been heard of in a country in which art had in any degree matured; Stuart was a very fair portrait-painter in the chalk and rose manner of the time; and West lived and worked in England to no very resplendent effect. Of sculptors and sculpture the record is barren.

With this cursory glimpse of the art of the American colonies we reach the threshold of modern art. The American and the French Revolutions had shaken the entire Western World to the foundations. The freedom man had struggled for throughout the ages seemed at last to be attained, but though there were, alas, many weary years to traverse before his goal could be reached, the shadow of these years did not fall athwart the smiling acres that lay between him and his new and far horizons. With high hope and confident courage he faced the coming years—and who shall say, as yet entirely in vain!

CHAPTER XXI

SOME TENDENCIES IN THE NINETEENTH AND TWENTIETH CENTURIES

The Renaissance Impulse Still Potent — The Cosmopolitan Tendencies of Modern Art — Official Recognition of Art in France — The Pre-Raphaelites in England — The Barbizon School — Sculpture — Greek Revivals in the United States — An American School in Architecture — The Artist and the Patron of Art — The World of Beauty.

IN the American and French Revolutions culminated those aspirations toward Liberty that are ineradicable from the soul of man. He had freed himself of his feudal overlords, had shaken off the gyves of priestly domination, and now he had refused further allegiance to kings and announced that thenceforward he would be self-governed. This was the goal toward which he had been blindly but instinctively moving for seven centuries. He had had to recover and assimilate all the lost learning of the antique world, develop and adapt its lessons to the problems of his own life, so different from that of the ancients and changing rapidly from decade to decade as the processes of thought became clearer and better organized. He had created new things in the arts as he had in politics and the science of life. After such creative periods, after the stress and tumult of action, there must be a recuperative pause.

I do not believe the tremendous force which called into being that which we name the Renaissance is by any means exhausted; the French Revolution is usually accepted as marking its end, and the beginning of the modern world; but I consider the Revolution merely an episode, merely a pause in the march of human progress, a pause to survey this freedom in which men in America and France faced the veil behind which lay their future—a future in which other thrones would fall and other men stand up as freemen with their destinies in their own hands for weal or woe.

We are yet too close to much that has gone on in architecture, painting, and sculpture, in the nineteenth and twentieth centuries to appraise it at its true values or to perceive clearly its true direction; however, one major tendency may be discerned—the art of the world is becoming cosmopolitan, losing its strongly marked national traits. This is readily explained not only by the conquest of those physical barriers to ready international intercourse to which I have so often referred, but also by the acknowledged leadership of France in the intellectual and artistic domain. America was an undeveloped wilderness and we were too busy conquering natural obstacles to give much thought to arts and letters. Italy, after giving modern music to the world, had sunk into an obscurity in which she labored to throw off the hateful yoke of the foreigner and take her place again. Neither England nor Spain could lead in art, and art in Germany might be said to be non-existent. This is particularly true of the first quarter of the nineteenth century.

It was only in France that art was a living and active force, and to her were turned the feet that in previous centuries would have journeyed to Rome. In her schools were trained the artists of Europe, and later those of America; the point of view of Paris prevailed and has continued to prevail. Hence, the effect of this common experience, this Gallic training, has been to draw together the sympathies of the artists of the Western world, give them a common point of view, and the strongly racial and national traits that had differentiated them before this cosmopolitanism

BOY WITH A SWORD, by EDOUARD MANET, one of the leaders of the Impressionist group, born in Paris, 1832, died 1883. It is difficult now to understand why such sympathetic and distinguished pictures as this were considered revolutionary sixty years ago.

A LANE IN THE WOODS, by JEAN BAPTISTE CAMILLE COROT, the poet of the dawn, born at Paris in 1796, and died, in 1875, at Ville d'Avray, where he had painted so many of his exquisite harmonies in silvery gray.

Detail of THE ANNUNCIATION, by SIR EDWARD BURNE-JONES, born at Birmingham, England, 1833, and died in 1898. A friend of William Morris, Dante Gabriel Rossetti, Ford Madox Brown, and others of the Pre-Raphaelite Brotherhood.

THE SOWER, by JEAN-FRANÇOIS MILLET, the principal figure of the Barbizon School, who found the motifs of his life's work among the peasants of France. He was born at Gruchy, near Cherbourg, in 1814, and died at Barbizon in 1875.

prevailed became so blurred that a Spaniard's work might easily be mistaken for that of a Frenchman, an Englishman, or an American.

The official school of art in France is the École des Beaux Arts. The system of instruction has a speciously democratic appearance concealing a very effective oligarchy. Study is carried on in a number of *ateliers*—workshops, studios— which may be organized by a group of students who request a distinguished artist to become their *patron* and visit their workshop once or twice a week to criticise their work. The studio is self-sustaining and self-governed, and the artist gives of his time and knowledge gratis in recompense for the pension and the honors he has in most cases received from the French Government. The great incentive in the studios of the École—there are many others outside of the School's sphere of authority—is the *Grand Prix de Rome*, whose winners each year in architecture, painting, sculpture, music, and engraving, go to the Villa Medici, maintained in Rome upon the Pincian Hill by the Government to pursue what we should call in America a postgraduate course of study; at the close of the term of four years they are given a post in France carrying a stipend with it that enables them to live modestly but relieved of the immediate necessity for earning their daily bread. Naturally, most of the *patrons* in the *ateliers* of the School have been holders of the *Grand Prix*. In order to win that prize their work must have conformed to official, academic standards and formulas in style, composition, color, even handling; the juries who judge the monthly competitions between the studios as well as those for the *Grand Prix* are composed of the *patrons*. It is easy to see that the result of such a system is to suppress or restrain exceptional and progressive talents and reduce them, if they will submit, to a general level, safe, competent in many ways, but cautious and conservative, certainly not, with the shadow of the academic fetiches of theme and treatment lying upon them, stimulating and inspiring. Beyond the *Grand Prix*, which is at once the guerdon of school work and the portal to a career, is the Institute of France, which may crown that career by admission to its sacred circle.

I have dwelt upon these details to explain the atmosphere in which the French artist has worked for so long; he has either ranged himself with the official, academic group, or has actively or tacitly opposed it and its teachings and ideals. The Annual *Salon* where the painters, sculptors, and architects exhibit their works—exhibitions of a magnitude unknown in America—are controlled by the official group, the exhibitions being held under governmental auspices. And this has accounted measurably for the rejection by the *Salon* juries of the work of men of such original force and genius as Jean François Millet, Edouard Manet, Claude Monet, and many others who declined to be governed by the opinions of academic mediocrities—of far more serious effect upon the fortunes of an artist than rejection by an American jury would have here; for there rejection means failure in the material sense and a restricted livelihood, acceptance means the seal of official approval and possible professional success. For artists must eat in order to live and work; they, like other men, desire the blessings of family life; and the story of the Millets' struggle with poverty is touching in its pathos and inspiring in its courage and devotion to an ideal.

Differences of opinion, disparate aims, opposing theories in color, composition, subject, treatment, form, surface, take on in such an atmosphere a vigor and bitterness that are extraordinary, and in the successive battles between the innovators—whether these be called Romanticists or Classicists or Orientalists or Realists or Impressionists or Cubists

The BURGHERS OF CALAIS, starved, ragged, and despairing, give up the keys of their city to the besieger. A composition which violates the theory, long held sacred, that a group must be built up in pyramidal form. Here is merely a file of awful presences returning slowly and sadly upon itself, in an arrangement unique in sculpture. It is by AUGUSTE RODIN, the greatest modern French master of sculpture, whose work ranges through realism, the idealistic, the dramatic, and the poetic.

JEANNE D'ARC, by EMMANUEL FREMIET, one of the modern masters of sculpture in France, born in 1824. The statue, in the Place des Pyramides in Paris, is in bronze, gilded, one of the most sympathetic of the many effigies of the Maid.

THE TRIUMPH OF THE REPUBLIC, in the Place de la Nation in Paris, by AIMÉ-JULES DALOU, born 1838, died 1902; one of the gifted group which, following Barye, broke with the stilted formulas handed down from the previous century.

or Futurists—and the conservatives of the moment is to be read the history of French art and, because of French leadership, the history of painting and sculpture in the nineteenth century.

In England the principal movement to record is that of the Pre-Raphaelite group, which sought a return to the simplicity of the early Italians before Raphael, as the name implies, led by Ford Madox Brown, Dante Gabriel Rossetti, Edward Burne-Jones, and William Morris.

In the youth of some of our own men, such for example as Frank Duveneck and William M. Chase, the school of Munich contributed to the formation of the taste and the direction of the thought of the American school that was slowly forming.

One of the notable tendencies in painting was the growing interest in landscape with or without figures. A remarkable group, of which Millet, Rousseau, Narcisse Diaz, and others were members, lived and painted at the little village of Barbizon, on the edge of the Forest of Fontainebleau, which gave its name to the group as the Barbizon school; they are often referred to as the men of 1830; and they were undoubtedly influenced by works of Constable exhibited in Paris in 1824–1825. With them Corot, that poet of the dawn and the silvery mists of France, may be ranged as friend and companion; Daubigny, also. They broke with the academic tradition, the confection of historical pieces, nudes, and compositions inspired by classical legend and the like, and found motifs for their masterpieces in the beauty of plain and forest and in the simple life of the peasant folk, epics of the forest, the river, seed-time, harvest, and the fold. And from these men derive a school of landscape-painters that gives promise of rising to great heights here in America and that has been distinguished by such names as Whistler, Inness, Homer, Wyant, Martin, and Murphy.

In the field of decorative painting in America the name of John La Farge is pre-eminent. A superb colorist, he has had an immense influence upon the American schools of design.

Of the next great group in France, the Impressionists, and their aims, we have given some account in Chapter VII of Part I. Their influence is potent in the work of to-day.

Of sculpture since the Revolutions one may say that the general tendency has been toward realism. In the early part of the eighteenth century the neo-Classic turn given to thought by the study of Roman institutions as a guide to life produced figures and groups conceived in what was believed to be the spirit of the antique, and called by all the sounding names of ancient story. But the work of such an epoch is doomed to oblivion if not to ridicule, for unless an art has its springs in the life of its own time it is dry, juiceless, barren. The drift of painting away from a pompous and lifeless academicism, in which classical story was warmed up for modern consumption very much on the model of the Academy of the Caracci, and toward that point of view which finds beauty and fit subjects for artistic treatment in the living world about us, had its counterpart in sculpture, and a strong school arose in France whose influence has spread and is brilliantly maturing in America. The names of Fremiet, Falguière, Dubois, Barye, and Cain are some of the jewels in that triple crown of the arts that France has worn so long.

Of the later French masters the work of Auguste Rodin marks a tendency and a leadership that may easily be fraught with danger—the danger that lies in the invasion of the field of a sister art, that of painting; for while some of his earlier

ork was extremely realistic—such for example as the fa-
nous figure which gave rise to the accusation that it was cast
om a living model, not modelled by the sculptor's hand—
s he grew older he drew farther and farther away from the
endition of actual form and became interested in the play
f light and shade that indicates form. This statement re-
uires some explanation. His Saint John gives every fact of
nuscle and sinew, of sun-dried skin stretched taut over the
ony frame, and the light and shade results from this real-
tic modelling. In such things as The Kiss and The Hand
f God the forms are modelled, not with reference to their
ccuracy as forms and to make the observer think pri-
narily of the forms, but are so handled, so softened, as to
reate the effect of a glamorous light and shade enveloping
he forms as a painter would be forced, by the limitations
f his means of expression, to treat them. The result in the
ands of this or any master is exquisite. But, as it was
vith Michael Angelo, danger lies in the exaggeration by fol-
owers of the master's personal vision and the neglect of
hat stern discipline by which a true master attains his
nastery of form and structure and his consequent right to
reat them as he will.

The strong interest that artists have taken of late years
n the solution of problems of light has thus reacted upon
culpture; and in painting, this interest, and that taken in
natters of technique, of the mere application of paint and
. neglect of design, is disquieting. The most brilliant im-
rovisation, the cleverest rendition of sunlight, firelight, or
amplight, cannot excuse the absence of those principles of
lesign that every work of art must respect.

In architecture in the United States we have had since
he Colonial period three separate revivals: the Greek Re-
ival, which filled the Eastern States, particularly New York,

with residences adorned with Grecian porticos of woo
and a simulation of the effect of smooth Pentelican marb
walls by the use of matched pine boards; the Gothic R
vival, of which Trinity Church in New York is an exempla
and the Classico-Renaissance Revival due to the turn giv
architectural thought by the World's Fair in Chicago
1893–1894. We have been afflicted also with sporadic a
tacks of originality which, like the Greek and Gothic R
vivals, withered because they had no roots in American so
A school of design that shall be firmly rooted in precedent-
I mean respect for the past as one respects one's father wit
out feeling it necessary to wear his garments—and base
upon the eternal principles of design, not upon the out
vesture given these principles by other nations in other tim
under other conditions of life and living, is yet to come b
is coming.

Here in America the danger lies in the tradition of imit
tion of the historic styles that has governed American d
sign. The teaching of the École des Beaux Arts, to whic
our architects owe so much, emphasizes the controlling i
fluence of the plan of a structure upon its interior and e
terior appearance, and the principle that from a new pla
suited to the functions of the building, from new groupin
of the several services, will result new masses and new fene
tration in elevation. Not only this, but the French arti
is free from the timidity that restrains the American fro
experiments in fresh ways to produce beautiful light an
shade in his mouldings and ornament. An examination
the work of the students of the École for the past centur
reveals a wonderful fecundity of idea and of resource i
these matters; that it usually lacks beauty and frequentl
scale in elevation is undeniable; but it has the equally und
niable virtue that is possessed by a living art striving t

PORTRAIT OF THE ARTIST'S MOTHER, by JAMES ABBOTT McNEILL
WHISTLER, called by him "Arrangement in Grey and Black," in the Luxembourg Gallery,
in Paris. In this picture Whistler rises to heights of distinction and shows a depth of tenderness unsurpassed by any other of his works. He painted many other portraits; and as a
landscapist, especially in his NOCTURNES, or night pieces, he reveals himself poet. He
was superb in water-color and pastel, and as an etcher is second only to Rembrandt.

JAMES ABBOTT McNEILL WHISTLER
Born at Lowell, Mass., 1834
Died 1903
Painted by William M. Chase

express a living and present civilization and to meet its needs material and æsthetic. In this atmosphere of logical plan and logical expression of plan the American architect who has had the privilege of that training steeps himself and, returning here, finds another tradition confronting him—the deplorable practice of first conceiving a building in terms of its exterior appearance, that exterior appearance being some example of some style of the historic past, and then fitting a plan, somehow, to that preconceived or borrowed exterior. He struggles against the tendency, but sooner or later succumbs in some measure to a practice he sees crowned on every hand with material reward and applauded by profession and public alike. Or, at the least, he yields to the drift toward the use of motifs ready to his hand in books instead of searching his mind for fresh and significant forms as he had done when he was a student. Architecture is unhappily the only art in which plagiarism is not considered disgraceful, is raised to the dignity of a fine art in itself, and receives the reward of a fine art for its successful practice. Luckily for the future of our architecture, however, the demands of the new problems, new buildings of new types, are forcing us to use merely borrowed garments from the fathers with which to clothe our native structural skeleton instead of borrowing the entire design bodily as the practice has been. The next step will be to give the same inventive thought to the clothing that is given to the practical requirements of the structure; and in this process of adaptation of the mouldings and ornamental motifs to new conditions of scale, relation, lighting, and character, something new will be gradually evolved, something eclectic, characteristic, national. In the speech of the undergraduate are always echoes of the last book he has been reading—and in the architecture of America the accent of the undergraduate is still to be discerned. But when the American architect has passed the architecture of the past through the crucible of his native genius, has laid aside his books, has learned to utter his own message eloquently and grammatically, there will arise on this continent an architecture thrilling in its dramatic quality, noble in its restraint and vigor.

"Westward the course of Empire takes its way." And with it Western art is destined to culminate in undreamed power and beauty, here, in the land we love.

Will you to whom this book is especially addressed, the future patrons and purchasers of painting and sculpture, the future builders of American architecture, be prepared to enjoy to the full this revelation of beauty when it shall come? The artist lives in an enchanted world of color and form, and the consciousness that this world is shut away from so many of his fellow beings fills him with regret, and the desire to share it with them. The pursuit of wealth, politics, civics, popular science, and sporst engross the American people to an extent unknown among the citizens of the Old World; one of the chief differences between the societies of Europe and America is that the European finds the time to enjoy the beauties of life as he goes, and comes to middle life with mind and soul nourished and enriched by thoughts beyond mere material things. The American public is frequently arraigned for making a god of business, because we are a commercial people, because the structures upon which the greatest pains and treasure are lavished are commercial buildings. Temples of Mammon, to use an evangelical turn of phrase. This is not entirely just, of course; it may be replied that the desire for wider markets sowed the seeds of Grecian culture along the Mediterranean littoral; the painting of Venice flourished with her trade; the spacious days of the Elizabethan era which gave us the art of Shakspere

THE CITY HALL in NEW YORK, designed by JOHN McCOMB, built in 1803–11, and showing the direct influence of the style of the Epoch Louis XVI, still current in that France with which our young country had such close and sympathetic relations. In this beautiful little building, in such admirable scale with the little town that was then New York, the seed of the Renaissance sown by Brunelleschi four centuries before blossomed in a land by him unknown, undreamed, beyond the Western Sea.

THE OPERA in Paris, designed by CHARLES GARNIER, built late in the reign of Napoleon III, one of the masterpieces of modern Renaissance architecture in France. In its masterly plan and its disposition of masses in elevation, it has been the prototype of many Opera Houses and Theatres in nearly every civilized country in the world. In its details it exhibits Garnier's predilection for the Néo-Grec, a style in which mouldings and ornaments are based on Grecian models, a mode he almost made his own.

were made possible by the wealth that England's ships brought home. The art of the world is nourished upon wealth, the wealth that should bring leisure in which to turn to things of the spirit. Every age has been a commercial age. Every age has had its share of the spiritual. And those in which commerce has flagged are also those in which the arts have failed to flourish. But the nation that puts commercial values above the spiritual, excludes beauty from its daily life, has not yet emerged from barbarism, or, what is worse, has sunk again to that level.

Steam-yachts, private cars, luxurious motors—what after all are these but highly developed means of comfortable transportation from place to place? And, as one moves in them through the world, what sort of world can it be that unrolls itself to a person ignorant of or insensitive to art or to the beauties of that Nature from which art extracts its rarest essence? To pass through cities rich in the architectural treasures of a thousand years, blind to their beauty and their meaning as records of a race seems incredibly stupid. To live in a formless, colorless world, bereft of pattern, of rhythm, of design, to be conscious merely of the difference between "bright" colors or "dull" colors but with no sense of their relations or harmonies or values, to be ignorant of the beauty of line and its sweep and movement and quality, of the cadences of great music, of the majesty of great literature—how hideous, how stupid, such a life and such a world must be!

If you would enter the world of beauty in which the artist dwells, enter by the artist's door. Look upon this bright and moving world in terms of Proportion, Balance, Symmetry, Rhythm, Pattern, Color, Harmony, Contrast, Beauty, as the artist does. The æsthetician who only writes of art is prone to ascribe to the craftsman in any art save literature all manner of ways of working and thinking that never enter the mind of the artist. The artist is trying to make something beautiful, and to accomplish that he combines selected elements of color and form and line and pattern or sound into a design; his attitude toward his work is just as simple and unaffected as that. And it is this simple attitude the artist invites the layman to share as the key to a true appreciation of art.

In the arts is most of the beauty of the world and of life in the world; they are for all men without even the asking; subtract them and the world is like a waterless desert.

Let us drink deep of the founts of beauty.

BIBLIOGRAPHY

Adam, R. and F., *The Architecture, Decoration and Furniture of*.
American Architect Series, *The Georgian Period*.
Anderson and Spiers, *Architecture of Greece and Rome*.
Ars Una. A Series of Monographs upon the Arts of the Countries of Europe.

Bannister-Fletcher, *A History of Architecture*.
Batifol, L., *Le Siècle de la Renaissance*.
Belcher and Macartney, *Renaissance Architecture in England*.
Berenson, B., *The Central Italian Painters of the Renaissance*.
  "   *The Florentine Painters of the Renaissance*.
  "   *The North Italian Painters of the Renaissance*.
  "   *The Venetian Painters of the Renaissance*.
Brownell, W. C., *French Art*.
Burckhardt, *The Cicerone*.
  "   *The Civilization of the Renaissance in Italy*.
Buschor, Ernst, *Greek Vase Painting*.

Carpenter, Rhys, *The Esthetic Basis of Greek Art*.
Choiseul, *L'Art de Batir chez les Romains*.
Committee on Education of the American Institute of Architects, *The Significance of the Fine Arts*.
Conway, Sir M. W., *The Van Eycks and their Followers*.
Cortissoz, Royal, *American Artists*.
Cram, Ralph Adams, *The Gothic Quest*.
  " " " *The Substance of Gothic*.

Dalton, C. M., *Byzantine Art and Archæology*.
Daly, César, *Les Styles Historiques*.
Dilke, Lady, *French Painters of the Eighteenth Century*.

von Fabriczy, *Italian Medals*.
Fromentin, E., *Masters of Other Times*.

BIBLIOGRAPHY

Gardens Old and New.

Gardner, Percy, *Greek Sculpture.*

Gasquet, *Henry VIII and the English Monasteries.*

Gillet, L., *La Peinture, XVII et XVIII Siècles.*

Gotch, *Early Renaissance in England.*

Gotch and Brown, *Architecture of the Renaissance in England.*

Guadet, *Elements et Théorie d'Architecture.*

Guerinet, *L'Archiiecture Française.*

In English Homes. A Series.

Isham, Samuel, *American Painting.*

Latham, *The Gardens of Italy.*

Letarouilly, *Edifices de Rome Moderne.*
"   *St. Pierre et le Vatican.*

Lethaby, *Westminster Abbey and the King's Craftsmen.*
"   *Mediæval Art.*

Lethaby and Swanson, *Church of Santa Sophia, Constantinople.*

Lubschez, Ben. J., *Perspective.*

MacColl, *Nineteenth-Century Art.*

Magonigle, *Architectural Rendering in Wash.*

Mâle, Emile, *Religious Art in France.*

Masters in Art, A Series of Monographs.

Moore, *Gothic Architecture.*

Morel, *Le Louvre et les Tuileries.*

Norton, *Church Building in the Middle Ages.*

Penrose, *The Principles of Athenian Architecture.*

Penty, *A Guildsman's Interpretation of History.*

Pfnor, *L'Epoque Louis XVI.*

Porter, *Mediæval Architecture.*
"   *Lombard Architecture.*

Prentice, *Renaissance Architecture in Spain.*

Prior, *Mediæval Architecture in England.*

Rivoira, *Lombardic Architecture.*

Rood, *The Book of Color.*

BIBLIOGRAPHY

Ross, *A Theory of Pure Design.*
" *The Painter's Palette.*
Ruskin, *The Stones of Venice.*

Saint, *Stained Glass of the Middle Ages.*
Strack, *Architettura Toscana.*
Street, *Gothic Architecture in Spain.*
" *Brick and Marble Architecture of the Middle Ages.*

Triggs, H. Inigo, *Town Planning.*

Villani, *Ancient Rome in the Light of Modern Excavations.*

Walsh, *The Thirteenth, the Greatest of Centuries.*

GENERAL

Adams, Henry, *Mont Saint Michel and Chartres.*
Atlas of Ancient and Classical Geography.
Bartholomew, *Literary and Historical Atlas of Europe.*
" *Literary and Historical Atlas of Asia.*
Baedeker, *Guide Books.*
Becker, *Charicles.*
" *Gallus.*
Bulfinch, *The Age of Fable.*
Carlyle, *The French Revolution.*
Cartwright, *Beatrice d'Este.*
" *Isabella d'Este.*
Cellini, *Autobiography, translation by Symonds.*
Guizot, *History of Civilization in Europe.*
Hegel, *Philosophy of History.*
Hewlett, *Little Novels of Italy.*
James, Henry, *A Little Tour in France.*
Lee, Vernon, *Euphorion.*
" " *Studies in the Eighteenth Century in Italy.*
Mahaffy, *Works on Greece.*
Meyer, *Ancient History.*
Michelet, *Modern History.*
Middleton, *Dictionary of Roman Antiquities.*

BIBLIOGRAPHY

Oliphant, *Makers of Florence.*
" *Makers of Venice.*
Pater, *Greek Studies.*
" *Studies in the Renaissance.*
" *Marius the Epicurean.*
Pausanius, *Description of Greece.*
Ranke, von, *History of the Popes.*
Scott, *The Architecture of Humanism.*
Sismondi, *History of the Italian Republics.*
Symonds, *History of the Renaissance in Italy.*
" *The Greek Poets.*
Taine, *English Literature.*
" *Philosophy of Art.*
Vasari, *Lives of Seventy of the Most Eminent Painters, Sculptors, and Architects.*
Wells, *The Outline of History.*

INDEX

Acropolis, Athenian, 7, 30, 73, 110, 114, 116, 120
Adam, Robert, 281
Alexandria, 122, 123, 124, 138; Library at, 123
Alexandrian Age, 30, 113, 115, 119, 122
Amboise, 224
America, 39, 140, 195, 223, 224, 240, 289, 292, 299, 300, 302, 305, 306
Amiens, 162, 165
Ammanati, 239
Apelles, 30, 46
Aphrodite Anadyomene, 120. *See* Venus Rising from the Sea
Aphrodite, Cnidian, 119. *See* Venus de Medici
Apollo Epicurius, temple of, 116
Appian Way, 137
Arnolfo, 188
Artemis, Temple of, 128
Artemis surrounded by her Nymphs, 120
Athene Parthenos, 44, 116. *See* Virgin Athena
Athene Promachos, 116
Athens, 4, 7, 44, 105, 114, 115, 116, 117, 118, 119, 120, 122, 123, 124, 138, 178

Barbizon, 299
Barozzi, Giacomo, 216
Barye, 300
Basilica at Pæstum, 113
Baths of Caracalla, 124, 137
Beauvais, 162
Bellini, 76, 212, 249
Bernini, 219, 231, 240
Blois, 236
Bonington, 91
Borgia, Cesare, 181
Botticelli, 187
Boucher, François, 4, 12, 15, 16
Boy with a Dolphin, 203
Brennus, 137
Brown, Ford Maddox, 299
Brunelleschi, Filippo, 177, 178, 188, 191, 196, 216, 235

Bullant, Jean, 236
Buonarotti, Michael Angelo, 4, 5, 8, 11, 15, 16, 26, 27, 76, 178, 187, 188, 191, 195, 196, 199, 204, 207–208, 211, 212, 215, 219, 246, 254, 265, 301
Burghers of Calais, 42
Burne-Jones, Edward, 299

Cagliari, Paolo, 212. *See* Veronese
Calumny of Apelles, 120
Campanile of Cathedral of Florence, 32
Cancellaria, 196, 199
Canova, 231
Caracci, 219; Academy of, 300; family of, 219, 246; Ludovico, 253
Caravaggio, 246, 253
Cassander, 123
Cathedral of Florence, Campanile of, 32
Cathedral of Santa Maria del' Fiore, 188
Cellini, Benvenuto, 30, 173, 224, 236
Cephisodotus, 119, 120
Chambers, Sir William, 281
Chambord, 236
Chardin, 86
Charles I of Spain, 224, 232, 261. *See* Emperor Charles V
Charles III, 266, 269
Charles VIII, 223, 224
Charles IX, 239
Chartres, 165; Cathedral of, 110
Chase, William M., 299
Choragic Monument, 123
Church of Santa Croce, 211
Church of Santa Maria Novella, 177
Cimabue, 31, 48, 177, 185, 188
City Hall of Paris. *See* Hôtel de Ville, 82
Cloaca Maxima, 137
Clodion, 254, 257
Cnidian Aphrodite, 119. *See* Venus de Medici
Colbert, 254
Colombe, Michel, 236
Colophon, 120

INDEX

INDEX

Gothic period, 158–169, 215, 277; English, 159, 161; French, 159, 161, 228
Goujon, Jean, 236, 254
Goya y Lucientes, 269
Gozzoli, Benozzo, 83
Grand Prix de Rome, 295–296
Greece, 7, 15, 30, 104–131, 132, 133, 134, 137, 138, 139, 144, 147, 153, 173, 178, 185, 186, 199
Greeks, The, 4, 7, 46, 48, 102, 104, 112, 133, 134, 139, 140, 153
Guizot, 166

Hals, Frans, 258
Hand of God, The, 301
Hardovin-Mansart, 240
Hawksmoor, Nicholas, 281
Hegel, 133
Hegias of Attica, 115
Hellenes, 104, 105, 127, 128, 132, 138
Henri II, 235, 236
Henri III, 235, 239
Henry IV, 235, 239. *See* Henry of Navarre
Henry VIII, 244, 277
Henry of Navarre, 235, 239. *See* Henry IV
Hera, 117; statue of, 117
Hermes, 7; with Infant Dionysus, 120
Hogarth, 281, 282
Holbein, Hans, 246, 254, 281
Hoppner, 281
Hôtel de Ville, 82. *See* City Hall of Paris
Houdon, 254, 257

Ictinus, 107, 116
Impressionists, 79–80, 286, 299, 300
Inness, 300
Innocent VIII, 200
Isabella d'Este, 200
Isabey, 91
Italians, The, 4, 137, 161, 182, 232, 235, 236, 239, 245, 262, 299
Italy, 15, 16, 105, 131, 132, 137, 140, 144, 147, 148, 149, 153, 154, 156, 157, 158, 161, 170, 173, 174, 177, 178, 185, 187, 188, 195, 200, 207, 212, 216, 220, 223, 224, 227, 228, 231, 232, 235, 240, 245, 253, 254, 258, 261, 262, 266, 269, 277, 278, 285, 289

Jones, Inigo, 278
Judgment Day, 155
Julius II, 199, 211

Kairos, 120. *See* Passing Opportunity
Kiss, The, 301

La Belle Ferronière, 203
La Farge, John, 300
Laocoön, 124
Laon, 165
Last Judgment, The, 8, 211
Last Supper, The, 203–204
Lawrence, Sir Thomas, 281, 282, 286
Lazzari, Bramante, 195, 196, 199, 204
Le Brun, 240
Le Nôtre, 240
Leopardi, Alessandro, 200, 215
Lescot, Pierre, 236
Le Vau, Louis, 240
Library, Sansovino's, 216
Lion Hunt, A, 258
Loggia of the Vatican, 203
Louis XI, 95, 223
Louis XII, 196, 224
Louis XIII, 235, 239, 240, 261
Louis XIV, *Le Grand Monarque*, 11, 12, 101, 219, 235, 240, 243, 244, 254, 270, 278
Louis XV, 12, 101, 243, 244; style of, 101
Louis XVI, 236, 269, 244, 273
Louvre, 124, 236, 239, 240
Luini, 249

MacNab, The, 285
Madonna in the Church of the Frari, 212
Magna Græcia, 113, 133, 138. *See* Greater Greece
Manet, Edouard, 79, 296
Mantegna, Andrea, 195, 196, 199, 200
Marbles, Elgin, 115
Martin, 300
Masaccio, 192
Mausoleum at Halicarnassus, 119
Medici, The, 208; tombs of, 211
Menander, 120
Millet, Jean François, 296, 299
Mnesicles, 110, 117
Mommsen, 133
Mona Lisa, 203
Monet, Claude, 79, 296
Morris, William, 299

317

INDEX

Moses, 211
Murillo, 53, 253
Murphy, 300

Naples Museum, The, 124
Narcisse Diaz, 299
Necho the Second, 102
Netherlands, The, 161, 224, 231, 253, 254, 265
Niké, 124. *See* Winged Victory
Niobe and her Children, 119
Notre Dame de Paris, 165

Olympia, 7, 116, 120, 127
Or San Michele, Saint George of, 191; Doubting Thomas of, 203
Ospedale degli Innocenti, 191

Palais de Justice, 165
Palais du Luxembourg, 239
Palazzo Pandolfini, 203
Palazzo Pitti, 191. *See* Pitti Palace
Palazzo Vecchio, 203
Palladio, Andrea, 216, 243, 278
Paris, 16, 124, 162, 165, 236, 240, 257, 261, 292
Parthenon, 7, 44, 107, 110, 113, 115, 116; frieze of, 44, 115
Passing Opportunity, 120. *See* Kairos
Periclean Age, 113, 115, 118. *See* Golden Age
Pericles, 4, 30, 113, 115, 116, 117, 118, 119, 178
Perrault, Claude, 240
Perugino, 200, 203, 249
Peruzzi, Baldassare, 203
Phidias, 4, 7, 15, 26, 30, 73, 110, 115, 116, 118
Phigalia, 116
Philip IV, 262
Piazza of Saint Peter, 219
Piazetta of Saint Mark, 216
Pilon, Germain, 236
Pintoricchio, 83
Piranesi, 281
Pisanello, 72
Pisano, 31, 188
Pisarro, 80
Pitti Palace, 239. *See* Palazzo Pitti
Poliziano, 207
Pompeii, 48, 113, 153; wall paintings of, 48
Poussin, Nicolas, 253, 258, 261, 262

Praxiteles, 4, 7, 15, 111–112, 119
Pre-Raphaelites, 299
Primaticcio, 224, 236

Raeburn, Sir Henry, 281, 282, 285
Rake's Progress, 282
Raphael (Raffaelo Sanzio), 4, 8, 11, 15, 16, 192, 195, 196, 199, 203, 204, 211, 249, 299
Realists, 296
Rembrandt van Rijn, 246, 254, 262, 265, 269
Renaissance, 4, 7, 16, 30, 31, 32, 44, 48, 71, 83, 100, 101, 137, 143, 153, 161, 165, 170, 177, 181, 182, 185, 187, 188, 191, 195, 196, 204, 207, 212, 220, 228, 231, 232, 235, 236, 245, 254, 257, 269, 273, 274, 277, 278, 289, 291
Reynolds, Sir Joshua, 281, 282
Rheims, 162, 165
Rhodes, 119, 124; Colossus of, 124
Ribera, 253, 261
Richelieu, 239, 240, 244. *See* du Plessis, Armand
Robusti, Jacopo, 212. *See* Tintoretto
Rococo, 219, 228, 265
Rodin, Auguste, 300
Romano, Giulio, 219, 249
Romans, The, 30, 128, 131, 133, 134, 137, 139
Romanticists, 296
Rome, 7, 8, 41, 114, 124, 128, 131, 132–143, 147, 148, 153, 178, 182, 186, 188, 192, 196, 199, 208, 216, 243, 249, 257, 258, 277, 281, 292, 295
Romney, George, 281, 282, 285
Ropps, 91
Rossetti, Dante Gabriel, 299
Rouen, 165
Rousseau, 299
Rubens, Peter Paul, 32, 246, 250, 253, 257, 261, 262
Ruskin, John, 286

Saint Benedict, 157
Saint Cecilia, 191
Sainte Chapelle, 165
Saint George of Or San Michele, 191
Saint John, 301
Saint John the Baptist, 203
San Gimignano, 182
San Lorenzo, 211
San Marco, 207, 216

INDEX

#50
50